Fighting Fantasy: dare you play them all?

FIGHTING FANTASY

THE DUNGEON ON
BLOOD ISLAND

IAN LIVINGSTONE

SCHOLASTIC

Published in the UK by Scholastic, 2024
Scholastic, Bosworth Avenue, Warwick, CV34 6XZ
Scholastic Ireland, 89E Lagan Road, Dublin Industrial Estate, Glasnevin,
Dublin, D11 HP5F

SCHOLASTIC and associated logos are trademarks and/or
registered trademarks of Scholastic Inc.

ISBN 978 0702 33860 1

A CIP catalogue record for this book is available from the British Library.

Printed in the UK
Paper made from wood grown in sustainable forests and other controlled sources.

MIX
Paper | Supporting
responsible forestry
FSC
www.fsc.org
FSC® C018072

3 5 7 9 10 8 6 4 2

www.scholastic.co.uk

Official FIGHTING FANTASY website www.fightingfantasy.com

CONTENTS

HOW WILL YOU START
YOUR ADVENTURE?

The book you hold in your hands is a gateway to another world – a world of dark magic, terrifying monsters, brooding castles, treacherous dungeons and untold danger, where a noble few defend against the myriad schemes of the forces of evil. Welcome to the world of **FIGHTING FANTASY!**

You are about to embark upon a thrilling fantasy adventure in which **YOU** are the hero! **YOU** decide which route to take, which dangers to risk and which creatures to fight. But be warned – it will also be **YOU** who has to live or die by the consequences of your actions.

Take heed, for success is by no means certain, and you may well fail in your mission on your first attempt. But have no fear, for with experience, skill and luck, each new attempt should bring you a step closer to your ultimate goal.

Prepare yourself, for when you turn the page you will enter an exciting, perilous **FIGHTING FANTASY** adventure where every choice is yours to make, an adventure in which **YOU ARE THE HERO!**

How would you like to begin your adventure?

IF YOU ARE NEW TO FIGHTING FANTASY...

It's a good idea to read through the rules that appear on pages 251–259 before you start.

IF YOU HAVE PLAYED FIGHTING FANTASY BEFORE...

You will know that before starting your adventure, you will need to roll dice for your character's Initial SKILL, STAMINA and LUCK scores. You can create your character by following the instructions on pages 251–259. Don't forget to enter your character's attribute scores on the *Adventure Sheet*, which appears on pages 260–271.

BACKGROUND

The fame and glory that Deathtrap Dungeon had brought Baron Sukumvit was something his brother, Lord Carnuss, just couldn't bear. People were in awe of the Baron and never stopped talking about his annual dungeon contest in Fang and the heroes who died trying to win the prize of 10,000 Gold Pieces. Lord Carnuss even sent his own battle-hardened champion to compete in the Trial of Champions, but he died a gruesome death, along with everyone else. One year, a brave Adventurer unexpectedly won through, so Baron Sukumvit rebuilt his dungeon and doubled the prize to 20,000 Gold Pieces, which simply added to his notoriety.

Whenever Deathtrap Dungeon came up in conversation, Lord Carnuss would fly into a rage, cursing his brother's name out loud. Over time, his jealousy turned into hatred. To upstage Sukumvit, Carnuss decided to build a dungeon of his own on Blood Island where he ruled and offer an even greater prize to the victor. That prize would be the Golden Orb of Fang, which he'd won from his brother in a dice game many years before. The Orb's value was difficult to estimate, but some say that, at auction in Shazâar, a bid of 25,000 Gold Pieces for such a legendary treasure would be the minimum expected. Carnuss revelled in the idea of offering a reward that was once his brother's prized possession. His plan was to hide the Orb deep inside the dungeon and protect it with deadly traps and ferocious monsters. He was certain the Orb would never be found. His message to contestants would be simple – find the Orb, escape from the dungeon, and the prize would be theirs to keep.

Carnuss built his dungeon by linking the underground caverns on Blood Island with a labyrinth of tunnels. Work began in secret, using an army of slaves. It took less than a year to build, but at a cost of nearly six hundred shackled souls. It was finished in time for the grand opening on the 31st day of Fire, just weeks before Baron Sukumvit's Trial of Champions took place in his reconstructed Deathtrap Dungeon.

Knowing his brother would be incensed by the news,

Carnuss sent a personal messenger to him, inviting him to enter a champion of his own to try to win back his precious Orb, or to just come as his guest to watch the greatest winner-takes-all tournament in Allansia. Outraged by his brother's attempt to usurp him by offering the Orb as a prize, Sukumvit sent the messenger back to Blood Island with an exceptionally rude note, written in blood, stuffed in the mouth of a dead rat.

Amused and encouraged, Carnuss sent word to all the towns in Allansia to announce that his dungeon on Blood Island would be open to all comers to win the Golden Orb. He chartered a fleet of boats to ferry contestants and spectators to the island from the mainland. He built taverns and rooms for spectators close to the Arena of Death where the contest would begin. News of the contest spread quickly. It soon became the talking point in every tavern and market square in Allansia. Adventurers, Warriors and Villains from far and wide bragged that they would go to Blood Island to win the Golden Orb.

YOU hear about the tournament on Blood Island from a merchant in Skaar, where you have come to sell a bronze sword that you found on an expedition to Kalong Marshes. With 5 Gold Pieces from its sale in your pocket, you are thinking about travelling to Fang to sign up for the Trial of Champions, but are intrigued by the new dungeon challenge on Blood Island. You walk down to the port where you see a crowd of people gathered in front of a small ship moored at the dock. The ship's captain is addressing the crowd, which is becoming increasingly noisy. 'This afternoon we sail to Blood Island where only the bravest Warriors will compete for the Orb!' he bellows. 'All you have to do to enter the contest to win Lord Carnuss's Golden Orb is step aboard my ship and sign up. And those of you who just wish to watch the contest, step on board and sail with us.'

Winning a prize worth 25,000 Gold Pieces seems unimaginable, and it's a challenge you cannot resist. Without further thought, you raise your arm and push your way through the crowd to walk up the gangplank to sign up for the contest. You are followed on board by a ruddy-faced Dwarf who also signs up to take the challenge. The captain shakes your hand firmly before welcoming more than fifty passengers aboard who want to witness the spectacle for themselves.

When the ship sets sail, all the passengers talk about is the dungeon and its monsters, and whether any of the contestants would survive. The Dwarf introduces himself to you as Thump and gives you a soft punch on the arm to emphasize his name. He's a stout man with a long beard and a studded iron helmet pulled down over his big bushy eyebrows. He's wearing a leather tunic and is holding a huge war hammer with a handle that is almost as long as he is. He tells you he comes from Stonebridge, a village that was almost destroyed by marauding Iron Giants. He says that if he won the Golden Orb, he would pay for Stonebridge to be rebuilt. He spends the voyage telling you tales of his many adventures, most of which seem wildly exaggerated. When you question him about his claim that he once killed a dragon with his bare hands, he leans back and roars, 'Well, maybe not entirely barehanded, but why spoil a good story with the truth!' Thump is a jovial, larger-than-life character and you can't help but like him, but it does feel slightly strange knowing that you will soon be competing with him for the Golden Orb.

Calm seas, a following wind and sunny skies make for a pleasant voyage, and when Blood Island is spotted on the horizon a loud cheer erupts on board. As the ship sails into the harbour, you see a large crowd of people waving from the dock, eager to see the new contestants. There's a carnival atmosphere with people laughing and cheering, trumpets blaring and drums beating loudly.

Standing on a platform is a tall, stocky man wearing long robes

Standing quietly surveilling the scene from a wooden platform set back from the crowded dock is a tall, stocky man wearing an elaborate headpiece and long purple robes filled out with huge shoulder pads. He seems to be quietly enjoying the moment. He is surrounded by stern-faced guards who push back anybody who tries to get too close to the platform. A trumpet sounds, and, when he raises his arms, the crowd falls silent.

The ship's captain orders you and Thump to follow him off the ship and walk through the crowd to the platform where the captain bows to the robed man. 'Lord Carnuss, I bring you two more contestants,' he says sharply. The robed man thanks the captain and glares at you and Thump before turning to address the throng. 'Citizens and honoured guests, I have good news to share with you. We now have 120 contestants ready to compete. I wonder which one, if any, will triumph?' he says, teasing the cheering crowd. He snaps his finger at a guard and growls, 'Feed and water these two wretches. They will need all their strength for the contest tomorrow.'

You are taken to a camp where groups of contestants are huddled together, talking. Some are practising their weapons skills; others are asleep, arms folded, leaning back against wooden cabins. They are a grisly mix of Warriors, Barbarians, Knights, Thieves, Ninjas,

Dwarfs, Elves, Man-Orcs, Pirates, Adventurers and Thugs who stare at you coldly as you walk into camp. Thump whispers in your ear, suggesting that the two of you should stick together, at least until the tournament starts. You spend the rest of the afternoon exercising and sharpening your sword. Thump swings his war hammer round his head and smashes it into the ground, practising the move many times. 'I think I'll use my war hammer to fight the next dragon I meet!' he says with a wink.

When the sun starts to go down, you are led to long wooden tables that are piled high with bowls of food. You sit down to a feast of vegetable soup, spit-roast chicken, grilled fish, cheese, fruit and honey. 'Enjoy your dinner!' a guard shouts out. 'It will probably be your last!' After the meal, you are taken to a log cabin, which you share with nine others, and told that you will be woken at sunrise to receive further instructions.

A bell tolls at dawn, and Carnuss's guards barge into your cabin, yelling at everybody to get up. When all the contestants are assembled outside, Lord Carnuss enters the camp and walks slowly up the steps of a small rostrum to address you. 'Welcome. Today is your day of destiny. Look around at your fellow contestants. Do they look stronger than you? Do they look quicker than you? Do they look smarter than you? Do you think you could defeat them in combat? As you can see, there are 120 contestants, all of you hoping to win the Golden Orb. Do you think that 120 contestants are too many to enter my dungeon? If you do, well, you are right! You will now be escorted to the Arena of Death where an elimination contest will take place. You will compete against one another until just twelve contestants remain who will have earned the right to enter my dungeon. I call it my Dungeon of Despair. It is filled with deadly creatures, lethal traps and horrific surprises,' he says with a beaming smile. 'Of the final twelve, eleven will most likely perish in the dungeon, and perhaps all twelve. But, with good fortune, wise decision-making and skilful combat, one of you might win through to claim the Golden Orb as your prize today. Be brave and be strong. May your swords be sharp and your wits sharper!' With his solemn words ringing in your ears, you watch Lord Carnuss leave the camp with his entourage following at a respectful distance.

YOUR
ADVENTURE
AWAITS!

May your STAMINA never fail!

NOW TURN OVER...

All the contestants are suffering badly in the heat

1

You are marched into the Arena of Death, which is a high-walled amphitheatre with a sand-covered floor and a bank of spectator seats circling the arena wall. With the spectator seats empty, an eerie silence prevails. The captain of the guard orders you to line up in twelve columns of ten. 'You will do everything I tell you to do. Stand to attention and do not move until Lord Carnuss is seated!' he shouts, barking out his orders. Without another word, he turns and leaves the arena.

The hours pass, but Lord Carnuss fails to appear. By mid-afternoon, the sun is unbearably hot, and you see that you are not the only one who is suffering in the heat. All the contestants are perspiring heavily, and some are swaying on their feet. You glance to your left and see Thump, who is grimacing but looking determined not to fail. You have a splitting headache, your mouth is bone dry, and you are desperate to quench your thirst. Lose 1 STAMINA point. If you want to take a sip of water from your flask, turn to **56**. If you want to remain standing to attention, turn to **323**.

2

As you approach the steps, you hear a whispering voice followed by sinister laughter. You stop and listen, but silence returns, only for the voice and laughter to begin again when you resume walking. When you reach the staircase, you hear a piercing scream as soon as your foot touches the first step. If you want to climb up the staircase, turn to **292**. If you want to go back and turn right at the junction, turn to **265**.

3

The narrow tunnel soon turns sharply left, and you walk along it for some distance in semi-darkness before it turns sharply right. You head east again, with the occasional screech of scurrying Rats breaking the silence, and eventually come to a junction. The tunnel carries straight on into the gloom as far as you can see. Looking left, you see that the tunnel soon ends at a doorway. There are burning torches on either side of the door, which you notice is covered with deep scratch marks. Curious, you decide to investigate. Turn to **48**.

4

A search of the room yields nothing else of interest other than a small copper charm in the shape of a beetle hidden in a crack in the wall. You may take the charm, and if you haven't done so already, you may look in the mirror (turn to **358**). If you would rather leave the room and walk along the corridor, turn to **331**.

5

You rummage through the Ratmen's pockets and find a piece of chalk, a glass eyeball, a small bottle labelled Weezle Juice, a small cat carved out of black marble and a chewed bone. After taking what you want, you set off again. Turn to **236**.

6

It's not long before the corridor ends at a T-junction where it joins a wide passageway. You look left and right and see nothing unusual or of interest. If you want to turn left and head west, turn to **70**. If you want to turn right and head east, turn to **215**.

7

You walk slowly along the tunnel, passing several more iron doors in the left-hand wall that are all firmly locked. You arrive at the end of the tunnel where there is another iron door. You try the handle, but the door won't open. *Test Your Luck*. If you are Lucky, turn to **137**. If you are Unlucky, turn to **288**.

8

You slide the irons bars to one side and open the door. You are almost trampled on by a huge CYCLOPS that pushes past you to get to the chest and empty it out on to the floor. The chest is full of rotten meat, which smells so bad it makes you retch. A cloud of Black Fly swarms out of the chest and buzzes round the Cyclops' head as it gorges on meat, oblivious to everything. If you want to go into the Cyclops' chamber, turn to **300**. If you would rather sneak out of the room and head north up the passageway, turn to **230**. If you want to leave the room and run back down the staircase and turn right at the junction, turn to **265**.

9

You wade through the murky water over to the left side of the cavern and climb the steps to enter the new tunnel and head north. Turn to **147**.

10

When you begin to speak, the Imp throws his head back and starts laughing hysterically. 'Talk? Talk? What is there to talk about? I just crashed my Spikle into the wall because of you. Give me a Gold Piece or I will summon somebody you wouldn't want to meet.' If you want to give the Imp a Gold Piece, turn to **81**. If you want to fight him, turn to **164**.

11

You try focusing on the words by holding the paper away from you, then closer to you, but still find it impossible to read. You put the paper in your pocket and look around the chamber. If you want to examine the objects on display, turn to **177**. If you want to walk over to the throne and pick up the Orb, turn to **228**.

You soon arrive at a cave with its entrance surround carved into the shape of two fire-breathing dragons locked in battle. Standing there, waiting to greet you, is Lord Carnuss, resplendent in his purple robes. A huge crowd of people has gathered at the entrance, with everybody jostling for position, desperate to see the contestants close up. Carnuss motions for the crowd to hush so that he can be heard. 'I congratulate the six finalists. You are all heroes, but alas, there can only be one champion. Now, I want each of you to stand on one of the slabs over here,' he says invitingly, pointing to six numbered stone slabs on the ground in front of him. The Assassin makes her mind up quickly and stands on slab number 1, followed by Caldwell, who steps confidently on to slab 3. Thump jumps on to slab 6 and motions to you to stand next to him on slab 5. If you want to stand next to him on slab 5, turn to **40**. If you want to stand on slab 2, turn to **316**. If you want stand on slab 4, turn to **176**.

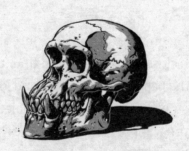

13

While the Troll Guard continues to insult you, you reach down and deftly slide the dagger out of your belt. You strike quickly, stabbing the Troll in the foot. He howls in pain and hops around on his other foot, cursing you. You seize your chance, grab your sword and run for the door at the back of the chamber. Turn to **392**.

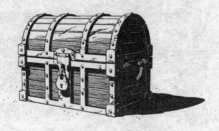

14

You manage to get both hands on the rope handrail and haul yourself back up on to the bridge just as a swarm of RATS appears from out of the west end of the tunnel. Not wishing to face hundreds of the creatures, you decide to try to leap over the invisible hole in the bridge. Much to your relief, you land safely on the other side and watch with satisfaction as the Rats run on to the bridge and fall down the hole into the ravine. Add 1 LUCK point. Relieved to have survived the illusion trap, you head off east down the tunnel. Turn to **174**.

A sickly gurgling sound erupts from the Zombie's throat

As they get closer, you see that the person is wearing armour that you recognize as belonging to one of the contestants. Although he is now wearing a chaos helmet that covers his eyes, you know it must be Caldwell, the Warrior-Knight. You call out his name, but he does not reply. He turns his head to one side at an odd angle as though he is listening for something. His body twitches occasionally, and you notice that he is walking erratically, stumbling slowly along. When he gets close, you see that some of the flesh on his face is missing, and yellow drool is dripping down from his broken jaw. A sickly gurgling sound erupts from his throat, and you realize that Caldwell has turned into a ZOMBIE and is lurching forward to attack you!

CALDWELL   SKILL 8   STAMINA 8

If Caldwell rolls a double during an Attack Round and wins the round, lose 2 additional STAMINA points caused by his Zombie bite. If you win, turn to **95**.

16

You are weak from holding your breath as you struggle to move inside the Glugg. Your skin feels like it is burning as the Glugg's gastric fluid starts to digest you. Lose 1 SKILL point and 4 STAMINA points. If you possess anything made of bronze, turn to **344**. If you do not have any bronze items, turn to **290**.

17

The Hobgoblin bites the Gold Piece before giving you the brass bell. 'You not me cheating,' he says, grinning. 'Not forgetting ringing bell when seeing Juggler Jak. If forgetting, him talking dopey and throwing stink at you!' The Hobgoblin makes a motion with his arm as though throwing a ball. 'Glass breaking. You snoring. Him stealing.' You thank the Hobgoblin for his advice, put the bell in your backpack and walk over to the archways. Turn to **393**.

18

The Dragonmaster stares at you from behind his mask for a while before saying, 'My instructions are that you cannot take the test without bone dice. But since this is the first test, I will give you the chance to win one of my dice. In return, you must give me all your food.' If you have Provisions and want to give them to the Dragonmaster, turn to **142**. If you want to attack the Dragonmaster, turn to **38**.

19

The Ghost-Witch stares at you and whispers coldly, 'Did you steal my cat?' If you want to reply 'Yes', turn to **160**. If you want to reply 'No', turn to **128**.

20

The Woodcutter nods his head in approval and says, 'Excellent. You have earned a reward.' He takes one of the hand axes off the wall and gives it to you. 'Listen carefully to the information I have for you. Further along this tunnel, you will come to a rope bridge over a narrow ravine. The bridge looks safe but it's not. It's an illusion. The middle boards are missing. If you walk across it, you will fall to your doom. I would advise you to jump over the ravine. It's not very wide. Now, I must ask you to leave as I still have lots of logs to chop up. I wish you good fortune on your quest.' With that, he opens the door, and you leave the room to carry on walking up the corridor. Turn to **386**.

21

As soon as you put on the armband, the door starts to swing shut. You dash for it and just make it through before the door slams shut behind you. The armband doesn't seem to have any magical properties, but it looks valuable. Turn to **249**.

22

Your arms ache painfully, but you somehow manage to keep the iron ball above your head. Without warning, the Ninja drops his iron ball, and screams angrily when it hits the ground. You drop your ball and sigh with relief as the Ninja is led away. You are exhausted after the ordeal and, worse still, the pain in one of your arms is getting worse. You have injured the shoulder of your sword arm. Lose 1 SKILL point and 1 STAMINA point. You are relieved to have won the contest and look around to see how Thump has fared. Turn to **310**.

23

You shout out to the Storeman, who wakes with a start and sits up, coughing and spluttering. He sees you and starts to panic. 'Don't attack me,' he pleads. 'I'm here to offer my goods to passing contestants. Everything you see costs 1 Gold Piece. I have lanterns, candles, rope, axes, leather gloves, water bottles, boots, hunting horns, canvas bags and Provisions. Take your pick.' If you want to buy any equipment or food, deduct 1 Gold Piece for each item and make a note on your *Adventure Sheet*. You say goodbye to the Storeman and leave the storeroom to head north. Turn to **116**.

24

It feels like there are two items in the bag: a small ball and a small cube. You loosen the string and empty the contents of the bag into your hand. They are a solid brass ball etched with a dragon motif and a bone die. You put both items in your backpack and decide what to do. If you have not done so already, you can either pick up the sword (turn to **345**) or, if you want to keep on walking, turn to **145**.

25

It's not long before you come to a large hole in the tunnel floor. There is a rope suspended from the ceiling that drops down into the hole and disappears into darkness. You tug on the rope, which feels like it would support your weight. If you want to slide down the rope, turn to **378**. If you want to walk past the hole and on up the tunnel, turn to **232**.

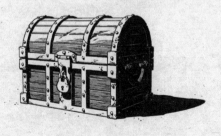

26

You jump to one side, but are hit in the arm by an arrow. Lose 2 STAMINA points. You look to your left and see that the Assassin has been struck by another arrow, this time in the stomach. It doesn't stop her, and she runs towards the Zanth Archers, ready to attack them with her spear. You charge at the archers who fired their arrows at you, striking the first one down before he has time to fire another arrow at you. You fight the other two one at a time.

First ZANTH ARCHER	SKILL 7	STAMINA 5
Second ZANTH ARCHER	SKILL 7	STAMINA 6

If you win, turn to **382**.

27

You wade knee-deep through the foul-smelling sewage water over to the stone steps, which you climb up to reach the door. It isn't locked, and opens into a long, dimly lit tunnel roughly carved out of the rock. The narrow tunnel is eerily quiet, and the air is cool and dank. You walk along the tunnel, which comes to a dead end at a locked iron door. Unable to open it, you walk back to the first door and down the steps. You walk along the ledge of the sewer in the direction of the slow-moving water and eventually see a speck of daylight in the distance. You soon arrive at the mouth of the tunnel where the sewage water pours out into the open sea below. You are trapped in the sewer, and with no way out, you have no option but to dive into the sea. You swim round to the harbour where you are hauled out of the water by guards and put on board a ship bound for the mainland. Your adventure is over.

28

The blade of the Vorpal Sword is heavy and sharp, causing large chunks of wood to splinter off the door. You manage to cut a hole large enough for you to climb through. You throw your backpack into the hole and dive after it with the ceiling just seconds away from touching the floor. Turn to **249**.

A Warrior woman is battling huge Spiders at the bottom of the pit

29

You walk through the doorway into a large room that has a silver chalice on a shelf on the far wall. A section of the stone floor in front of it has given way to reveal a deep pit. You walk to the edge of the pit and see a Warrior woman in leather armour at the bottom. It's Azurra Xang, the Assassin. She is frantically stabbing huge black SPIDERS with bodies the size of coconuts with her spear as they pour out of a large pipe protruding from the pit wall. She looks up and glowers at you without saying a word. If you want to help her climb out of the pit, turn to **260**. If you would rather leave her to fend for herself and take the silver chalice, turn to **396**. If you would prefer to leave the room immediately and walk on, turn to **124**.

30

You search through your backpack and find the tin. You begin to feel unwell as you prise the lid off and rub the brown, foul-smelling paste on to your wound. Much to your relief, the paste works immediately, killing the Parasites in your blood before infection takes hold. Add 1 STAMINA point. You look around and see a tunnel heading east out of the cavern. Turn to **3**.

31

You scan the shelves quickly and see spell books, treasure books, history books, mythology books, books of maps, books of monsters, books on the undead, books on the heroes of Allansia, books of artefacts, books of potions and more. There are hundreds of books in the library of which three titles intrigue you the most. Will you:

Open the book entitled
Dead and Undead?   Turn to **248**

Open the book entitled
Mages and Magic?   Turn to **263**

Open the book entitled
Dungeon of Despair?   Turn to **152**

Leave the library and
continue up the corridor?   Turn to **179**

32

You search the cave and discover a large tunnel entrance at the back of the cave that has been blocked up with boulders and rocks. The only way out of the cave appears to be the iron door you came in from. You bang on the door with the hilt of your sword and are relieved to see it open. The Dragonmaster beckons you back into his chamber and tells you to stand in front of his table. 'You did well to survive,' he says in his cold voice. 'Your final task is to unlock the door behind me. Did you find any gold Compass Keys in the dungeon? If so, place them on the table.' If you possess any numbered gold keys and want to put them on the table, turn to **239**. If you want to tell the Dragonmaster that you do not have any Compass Keys, turn to **148**.

33

You are soon back at the junction, where you decide to head straight on. The roughly hewn tunnel walls become smoother and are interspersed with carvings of dragons and demons. The floor has a layer of sand on it with fresh footprints heading west. It's not long before the tunnel curves slowly round to the right, and, as you continue on, you hear the high-pitched laughter again. Suddenly a large, iron-rimmed wooden wheel with pyramid-shaped spikes comes hurtling round the bend at high speed. The wheel has footholds on the inside like a giant treadmill and is being ridden by a small green-skinned creature with a wide mouth, wild eyes, pointed ears and a long ponytail trailing behind him. It's a wicked IMP, and he is laughing manically as he steers his Spikle straight at you! Roll two dice. If the total is equal to or less than your SKILL score, turn to **286**. If the number is greater than your SKILL score, turn to **303**.

34

You climb up the steps as the GHOST-WITCH glides down silently until she stops no more than two steps away. You see that her feet are not touching the ground, but you sense that she is very real. She hovers over you, her head tilted to one side, with a wide-eyed, sickly grin on her face. 'You have not run away from me. How very kind of you,' she says in a scratchy voice, staring straight at you without blinking. 'I would be so lonely down here if it were not for my little cat Lawrence. He's so sweet. But I've lost him. I was reading in the library, and suddenly he was gone. Have you seen him?' If you want to reply 'Yes', turn to **156**. If you want to reply 'No', turn to **297**.

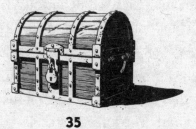

35

The Barbarian's feet slide out from under him, and he falls on the ground. Before he can stand up, your opponents seize their chance and give the rope a mighty heave, which pulls your team forward by half a metre. You yell at your team to lean as far back as possible with their legs straight out. Roll two dice. If the total is equal to or less than your SKILL score, turn to **102**. If the number is greater than your SKILL score, turn to **349**.

36

You check the throne carefully for hidden traps, but don't find any. If you want to pick up the Orb, turn to **228**. If you want to search the chamber, turn to **343**.

37

The Woodcutter sees you reach for your sword and quickly grabs two of the hand axes from the wall. Twirling the axes through the air, he steps forward to fight you.

WOODCUTTER   *SKILL* 6   *STAMINA* 5

If you win, turn to **374**.

38

When the Dragonmaster sees you draw your sword, he raises his right arm and points at you. A jagged bolt of lightning flies out from the ring on his finger and slams into your chest. The force of it sends you flying, and you smash your head against the back wall. Wracked with pain and barely able to move, you can do nothing but watch the Dragonmaster pull down a lever on the wall to open a trapdoor. He grabs your legs and drags you over to the trapdoor and pushes you down a chute. As you slide down, you hear him shout, 'Be gone with you!' Turn to **214**.

39

You sheathe your sword and walk down the steps to where the tunnel runs down to a dark, flooded cavern. The water looks jet black, with streaks of red luminescence caused by BLOODWORMS swirling around on the surface. All is quiet except for the sharp echo of water droplets falling from stalactites into the water below. The silence is suddenly broken by a piercing screech. A grotesque four-armed creature emerges from the gloom, striding quickly through the shallow water towards you. It has thin, pallid skin stretched over its large skull, and long spines protruding from its shoulders and down its back. It screeches again, louder this time, with its four arms raised, ready to attack. The creature is a HOWLING DEMON, and, as it closes in on you, its howls become terrifyingly loud. If you have drunk a Potion of Mind Control, turn to **283**. If you have not drunk this potion, turn to **118**.

40

You stand on the slab and watch the Monk stand on slab 2 and finally the Thief, who cautiously steps on to slab 4. Your heart begins to pound in your chest when Carnuss reaches for an iron lever protruding from the wall of the cave entrance. The crowd goes silent when he takes hold of it with both hands. 'Contestants, you are about to enter my Dungeon of Despair. When I pull down on this lever, you will drop through the floor. I should warn you that one of you will not survive the fall! If any of you want to change places with another contestant, do so now!' The Thief raises his hand and says, 'I'll swap if anybody else will?' The Assassin quickly agrees to swap slabs with the Thief, who seems to be enjoying himself. Now standing on slab 1, the Thief says jovially, 'Anybody else want to switch slabs?' If you want to change places with the Thief, turn to **299**. If you want to stay where you are, turn to **93**.

41

You check the box for traps, and, satisfied there isn't one, you slowly lift the lid. Inside, you find a silver key lying on top of a red silk cushion. Add 1 LUCK point. You take the key and await your next instruction, but the room remains silent. If you want to open another box, turn to **388**. If you want to open the door, turn to **165**.

42

The Gatekeeper nods his head and hands the Orb back to you. 'Congratulations,' he says with a wry smile. He takes a key out from under his robes, unlocks the bronze door and pushes it open. You breathe in deeply and walk out into bright sunshine to be met by a deafening roar. Turn to **400**.

43

Further along the tunnel, you stop to look at a large hole in the ceiling when you suddenly hear loud, stomping footsteps coming down the tunnel. You draw your sword and stand ready to face the oncoming creature. Turn to **261**.

44

You place your sword in the box and stoop down and walk through the archway. You follow the tunnel east until it makes a sudden left turn. You head north and walk on for fifty metres to where the tunnel comes to a dead end. There are two huge white clay hands with black-painted fingernails attached to the end wall. The left one is held out with its palm open, and the right one is a clenched fist holding a scroll. There is a sign on the wall, written in what looks like dried blood, which says, 'Pay 1 Gold Piece, no more, to learn the secret of the Dragonmaster's door.' If you want to place 1 Gold Piece in the palm of the hand, turn to **103**. If you want to try to pull the scroll out of the clenched fist, turn to **306**.

45

You put the key in the keyhole and hear a satisfying click as it turns in the lock. You open the door and step through into a long, dimly lit tunnel heading north. As you walk along in semi-darkness, you do not see a tripwire stretched across the passageway. *Test Your Luck*. If you are Lucky, turn to **274**. If you are Unlucky, turn to **321**.

46

You watch the coin land on the floor. It's a head. When you reach down to pick it up, you hear the noise of coins jingling behind you. You look inside the box and find a leather purse that contains 3 Gold Pieces. You take the coins and continue on up the passageway, pleased with your reward. Turn to **348**.

47

When all the contestants have chosen their partners, the officer makes an announcement. 'Bull's Eye is an archery contest. I hope you have chosen wisely because the targets for this contest are you, the contestants!' He sniggers, hardly able to contain himself. The spectators gasp when they hear his words. You know that High Elves are excellent archers and look over to see that she is smiling confidently. 'Form yourselves into two lines of fifty-five contestants, making sure you stand opposite your partner, thirty paces apart. You will be given a bow, and you must fire an arrow at your partner when you hear the trumpet sound. Anybody who is hit by an arrow will be eliminated, some fatally so.' You take your place in the line opposite the High Elf. Guards enter the arena to hand out the bows and arrows to the contestants. When you see the Elf's arrow aimed straight at you, you breathe in deeply and take aim at her. The crowd roars at the sound of the trumpet and you release your arrow. Roll two dice. If the total is higher than the High Elf's SKILL of 8, turn to **117**. If the total is 8 or less, turn to **389**.

The gauntlets have sharp steel spikes and fingertips

48

You examine the door and see that the scratch marks have been made quite recently. You try to open the door, but it is locked. You sense something is behind you and turn round to see a pair of steel gauntlets hovering in the air, moving slowly towards the door. The gauntlets have sharp spikes on the back, and fingers ending in pointed steel tips that look like long fingernails. If you want to grab hold of the gauntlets, turn to **208**. If you want to step to the side to let the gauntlets reach the door, turn to **253**.

49

The blade of your hand axe is blunt and makes little impact on the solid oak door. The ceiling continues to grind its way down the walls and there is nothing you can do to stop it. You try standing your sword upright on its tip on the floor, but the blade snaps under the weight of the ceiling. There is no way to escape being crushed. Your adventure is over.

50

The door is firmly locked. If you have a bronze key, turn to **277**. Or, if you have not done so already, you can slide open the peephole in the door (turn to **370**). If you don't have a bronze key and want to set off again, turn to **236**.

51

The door opens into a small room where you see a little old man cowering in the corner. He looks terrified. 'Don't attack me! Don't attack me,' he whimpers. 'I'm here just to look after the Lord Carnuss's paintings in the hallway. That's all I do. Nothing more. As you saw, he's a very good artist, but doesn't want everybody seeing paintings of his brother being savaged by monsters! I can't sell you a painting, but I can sell you an old ring I found. Give me 1 Gold Piece and it's yours. It looks like a magic ring to me.' If you want to buy the ring, turn to **167**. If you want to leave the room and open the door at the end of the corridor, turn to **309**.

52

You are exhausted after the long battle and are breathing heavily as you scramble over the carcass of the Raptorex. You walk on along the tunnel for some distance and are stopped in your tracks when you see a body lying face down in a pool of blood up ahead. For a moment, you think it is Thump, but when you get closer you see it is the mangled remains of a Goblin who must have been attacked by the Raptorex. A quick search of the Goblin's pockets yields a copper bracelet and some broken teeth. You throw the teeth away and examine the bracelet. There are mysterious runes etched on the inside. If you want to try on the bracelet, turn to **313**. If you would rather put it in your backpack and set off again, turn to **158**.

53

The Orc Skeleton does not move when you slide the silver armband off. You see it is intricately engraved with mysterious runes. If you want to put the armband on, turn to **21**. If you want to leave the room without it, turn to **249**.

54

You pour the oil on to the palm of your hand and start rubbing it on the bites that are now red and angry and are beginning to swell. The oil acts quickly and calms the swelling, and it doesn't take long for the itching to stop. Feeling calmer, you look inside the chest and see a finely crafted breastplate made of polished steel. If you want to try on the breastplate, turn to **204**. If would rather walk back down the tunnel to the T-junction, turn to **33**.

55

The Dragonmaster points to himself and says, 'I win. You have failed in your quest, but, thanks to the generosity of the great Lord Carnuss, your life will be spared for being the first contestant to get to this point.' The Dragonmaster pushes a lever down on the wall behind him, which opens a trapdoor in the floor above a chute. He tells you to slide down the chute, adding, 'Freedom awaits you.' If you want to slide down the chute, turn to **214**. If you want to attack the Dragonmaster, turn to **38**.

56

You reach down for your flask and are immediately set upon by two guards who beat you to the ground with their wooden staffs. Lose 2 STAMINA points. 'Stand to attention and do not move again until you are told to do so!' one of them screams at you angrily. You pick yourself up and resume your standing position with your headache now worse than ever. Turn to **323**.

57

You pull down on the lever and hear the rattling sound of chains in the distance followed by a dull grating sound. The grating sound gets louder and louder, and, seconds later, you see a giant dragon skull made of stone sliding down the tunnel at high speed towards you. There is nowhere to take shelter. You turn and run, but cannot escape from being run down and squashed by the giant skull. Your adventure is over.

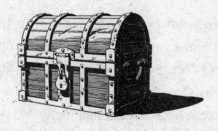

58

You sit down in the chair, expecting a charge of energy to surge through your body, but seconds later you feel incredibly tired. You are unable to keep your eyes open and fall fast asleep. You are asleep for only a few seconds before your eyes pop open. You stand up, feeling strong and completely refreshed. Add 1 SKILL point and 2 STAMINA points. You stride up the tunnel and soon arrive at a junction. The new tunnel in the left-hand wall is narrow and has a very low ceiling. There is a terrible smell of rotten eggs coming from it and you decide to walk straight on. Turn to **115**.

59

The Goblin's aim is poor and his dagger flies harmlessly past you. Before he has time to throw another dagger at you, you run forward and launch a double-footed dropkick at the Goblin that sends him and his fellow guard tumbling down the stairwell, screaming loudly. You run down after them and find them both lying unconscious on the cavern floor. You rummage through their belongings and find two throwing daggers, a brass button, a small bottle of Mullweed Oil, a rabbit's-foot charm and a piece of stale bread. You eat the bread (gain 1 STAMINA point) and take what items you need before walking through the archway into the tunnel to head east. Turn to **207**.

60

You stand in front of the marble throne and press down gently on the dragon eyes. A section of the wall swings out to reveal a narrow passageway. If you want to pick up the Orb, turn to **228**. If you want to enter the passageway without the Orb, turn to **242**.

61

You are temporarily blinded by the searing rays of light. You hear the door open and close again, and the high-pitched sound of squeaking voices. You can just make out the blurred outline of two creatures standing in front of you with their long whiskered snouts poking out of their hooded robes, and you fumble for your sword to defend yourself. They are RATMEN armed with short swords, and you must fight them one at a time. Reduce your Attack Strength by 3 during each Attack Round for this battle only.

First RATMAN	SKILL 5	STAMINA 5
Second RATMAN	SKILL 5	STAMINA 4

If you win, turn to **163**.

A creature with spike-covered hide bounds up the steps on all fours

62

The tunnel continues straight on, and eventually ends at a flight of stone steps that curve round to the right. You hear footsteps coming towards you at speed and draw your sword. A burgundy-coloured creature with a spike-covered hide comes flying round the bend and bounds up the steps on all fours with its red eyes fixed firmly on you. It doesn't stop, and leaps at you, slavering at the mouth. It is a vicious THORN DEMON, and you must fight it knowing that one bite of your flesh could be fatal. If you are fighting with a Vorpal Sword, add 2 points to your Attack Strength during each Attack Round for this battle only.

THORN DEMON   *SKILL* 10   *STAMINA* 8

If you win but lose one or more Attack Rounds during combat, turn to **140**. If you win without losing any Attack Rounds, turn to **39**.

63

Weakened by the poison, you must decide what to do. If you want to try to grab the glass object on the floor before you climb up the ladder, turn to **171**. If you want to climb up the ladder straight away to open the door, turn to **110**.

64

The Dwarf thanks you for the food and eats it quickly. He lets out a huge belch after he's finished eating and wipes his mouth with the back of his hand. 'That's better!' he says contentedly. 'Now, let me give you something in return.' He opens his leather bag and pulls out a small magnifying glass. 'I have a feeling you might need this,' he says, handing it over to you. 'This tunnel comes to a dead end so you might as well turn round and walk back with me. I'm going to try again to find a way out of this infernal dungeon.' You are soon back at the copper mouth entrance where you shake hands and say goodbye. 'Toodle-oo!' Diggle says cheerfully, and turns left to head south, mumbling to himself. You turn right and head north up the passageway. Turn to **138**.

65

The tunnel eventually ends at a set of double doors. The Assassin runs ahead to listen at the doors. She looks back at you and shakes her head to signal that she can't hear anything. You draw your sword and watch her carefully open one of the doors and step through. She suddenly falls back through the door, holding her shoulder where an arrow is lodged. Turn to **298**.

66

You say the words softly and almost immediately one of the panels in the bookcase set against the far wall begins to slide forward. There is an alcove behind the bookcase where you see a small wooden box on a stone shelf. You shake the box and hear something rattle inside. If you want to open the box, turn to **192**. If you want to leave the box on the shelf, and you have not done so already, you can either open the book entitled *Dead and Undead* (turn to **248**) or open the book entitled *Dungeon of Despair* (turn to **152**). If you want to leave the library and continue up the corridor, turn to **179**.

67

You take the iron key off the back of the door and put it in the lock. The key turns and the padlock pops open. You place the key in the second padlock, which also opens. You put the key in your pocket just as somebody suddenly starts thumping violently on the other side of the door. 'Meat! Meat! Give me meat!' an angry voice booms out. If you want to unbolt the door, turn to **8**. If you want to leave the door bolted, and you have not done so already, you can either eat the bread and cheese (turn to **168**) or open the chest (turn to **385**). If you would rather leave the room and head north up the passageway, turn to **230**. If you want to leave the room and run back down the staircase and turn right at the junction, turn to **265**.

68

You think back to when you left the Assassin in the Spider Pit and stay silent. 'Lost your tongue?' she calls out menacingly. 'What goes around comes around, so don't expect any help from me. Think yourself lucky you are not sharing the pit with poisonous Spiders. Anyway, I must be going. It was nice not talking to you!' You watch her leap over the pit and disappear. You run your fingertips over the walls, searching for a crack or a secret door, but do not find anything. You sit down to rest, and, as the hours go by, you begin to lose hope. You stand up when you hear voices, but soon realize that they are not speaking a language you understand. Several heads appear over the edge of the pit. It's a patrol of ZANTH ARCHERS. They get very excited and draw their bows and fire down at you. Your adventure is over.

With the Man-Orc slain, you watch the final battle, which ends with the Barbarian slumping to the ground. All the spectators rise to their feet to applaud the victors. Even Lord Carnuss stands and claps. You are exhausted but relieved to have survived the elimination contest. While the spectators begin to make their way to the dungeon to watch the start of the contest, you look around the arena and see that the victors are the Monk, the Warrior-Knight, the Thief, the Assassin and Thump who punches the air triumphantly. You are led out of the arena by the officer and taken to a small building nearby to rest and eat. Add 2 STAMINA points. Nobody is talking and you decide to break the silence and introduce yourself to the others. The Thief bows and says, 'Greetings. Fingers Foley is my name, and thieving is my game. In case you were wondering, I was given the nickname "Fingers" not because it's a thief's name, but because my little finger was cut off as punishment for sneaking out of the Black Lobster tavern in Port Blacksand without paying for my drinks. I usually get away with it, but not in Port Blacksand.' Thump asks him how he was able to defeat the Priestess. 'Oh, that was easy. I didn't lose my thieving skills when I lost my finger! As we chatted while walking across the arena, I slipped her magic ring off her finger without her noticing! You should have seen the look on her face when she realized what I'd done!' The Monk is called Uzman Koh and says he is from Fang.

'Sukumvit raged for days when he heard about his brother's dungeon. Silly old fool!' he scoffs, leaning on his staff. The armoured Warrior-Knight is from Chalice and goes by the name of Caldwell. He is man of few words and looks to be quietly assessing everyone's strengths and weaknesses. The last contestant is Azurra Xang from Zengis. 'Watch your back. I'm an Assassin,' she says mischievously with a sly smile. Trumpets suddenly blare to signal that it is time for you to enter Carnuss's Dungeon of Despair. As you get ready to go, Thump whispers in your ear, 'Shall we make a pact not to fight each other in the dungeon?' If you want to make a pact with Thump, turn to **195**. If you do not want to make a pact with Thump, turn to **368**.

70

You set off west and notice that the passageway becomes wider, and the ceiling becomes higher. The passageway soon makes a sharp right turn, and you walk north for a while before arriving at a doorway in the left-hand wall. There are bloody footprints in front of the door and the handle is covered with fresh blood. If you want to open the door, turn to **359**. If you want to press on, turn to **154**.

71

Seeing nobody beyond the archway, you step through it and walk down the tunnel, passing the Warrior-Knight's body, before reaching the junction where you continue west. Turn to **80**.

72

The door opens into a small room that has bare stone walls except for the back wall, which has a row of axes hanging on nails. There is a small table in the corner with a large burning candle in a bottle, and a small, stoppered clay pot on top. In the middle of the room, standing in front of a large pile of logs, there is a long-haired, bearded man with his shirtsleeves rolled up who is busily chopping wood. His axe is sending wood chippings flying everywhere. He is focused on his task, and he doesn't look up when you enter the room. If you want to talk to him, turn to **295**. If you want to leave the room and carry on walking up the corridor, turn to **386**.

73

The Vampire Bat that bit you on the neck was not carrying any Parasites. You look around the cavern and see a passageway heading north out of it. Turn to **3**.

74

You dive down, but the Lava Demon's aim is true, and you are hit in the side by the ball of lava. The pain is intense, but you manage to scrape the lava off your skin with your sword. Lose 1 SKILL point and 6 STAMINA points. If you are still alive, you see the Lava Demon reaching down to pick up another handful of lava. You grit your teeth and stand up and run as fast as you can along the pathway round the fire pit into the new tunnel. Turn to **129**.

75

The Thief looks disappointed that nobody wants to change places with him, but he shrugs his shoulders as though he doesn't care. The crowd gasps when Lord Carnuss suddenly pulls down on the iron lever and the slabs fall away. You drop through a hole and find yourself sliding down a stone chute, landing with a splash into a stinking sewer. Lose 1 LUCK point and 1 STAMINA point. Pale light from amber crystals fixed to the walls reveals stone steps further along the sewer that lead up to a door in the wall. Looking the other way, you see several pairs of glowing red eyes in the distance that are slowly advancing towards you. If you want to wade through the foul-smelling sewage over to the steps to open the door, turn to **27**. If want to wait to find out what creatures are approaching, turn to **355**.

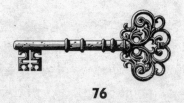

76

You search through your backpack and pockets, but cannot find an iron key. The Gnome sighs and says, 'Thank you for trying. Maybe somebody else will have one. If you were thinking of going north, don't. There's a lethal trap up ahead.' If you want to carry on heading north, turn to **247**. If you want to take the Gnome's advice and turn round, turn to **375**.

77

You head east and turn the corner to head north where the tunnel floor is bare stone, and the footprints are no longer visible. You see two magnificent oak chairs set opposite each other against the tunnel walls. They both have signs above them with the words 'Healing Chair' written in red ink. If you want to sit down on the chair set against the left-hand wall, turn to **225**. If you want to sit down on the chair set against the right-hand wall, turn to **58**. If you want to keep on walking, turn to **399**.

There is a bronze statue of a Warrior looking to pick up a ring

78

You pick up the sword that is radiating shades of blue light. It is a powerful Vorpal Sword that is imbued with magic. If you wish to take the Vorpal Sword, you must leave your own sword behind. You set off again and go down the stone steps. The tunnel soon turns left, and you head west for a while before coming to another junction. The tunnel carries straight on into the gloom as far as you can see. Looking right, you see that the tunnel soon ends at a doorway. There are burning torches on either side of the door, which you notice is covered with deep scratch marks. Curious, you decide to investigate. Turn to **48**.

79

The door opens into a small room that has smooth stone walls and a flagstone floor. On the far wall, there is a large, cracked mirror in a gilt frame of elaborately carved snakes, and in the centre of the room there is a bronze statue of a Warrior bending down as though he is about pick up the silver ring that is lying on the floor. Will you:

Look in the mirror?	Turn to **358**
Pick up the silver ring?	Turn to **126**
Close the door and walk up the corridor?	Turn to **331**

80

The tunnel continues straight on, and you see nothing of interest until you come to the edge of a pit spanning the width of the tunnel. You cannot see the pit floor as it is covered by a seething mass of large Cockroaches crawling over each other. There is a frayed rope hanging from the ceiling over the pit. If you want to jump down into the pit and stride through the Cockroaches to the other side, turn to **119**. If you want to jump on to the rope and swing over the pit, turn to **308**.

81

The Imp looks a little surprised when you hand him the Gold Piece, but he says nothing and puts it in his pocket. You watch him dash over to his Spikle to examine it for damage. He picks it up and steps inside the wheel. 'What luck. It's not damaged at all,' he says sarcastically. He scoots off and disappears round the bend heading east. 'I'll get you again on the way back, wormbrain!' he shouts and starts laughing hysterically. The laughter soon dies away, and you set off again, now heading north. Turn to **104**.

82

You unlock the door and walk out of the room into a narrow corridor. You look right and see that the corridor soon ends at a blank wall. You look left and see that the corridor heads north for a while before turning left. You decide to go north, turning left and heading west until you come to a junction. Looking straight ahead, you see that the corridor carries on for some distance into the gloom. Looking right, you see there is somebody up ahead lying on the floor, propped up against the wall, groaning. He is holding a war hammer on his lap. It's Thump! If you made a bond with Thump, turn to **233**. If you did not make a bond with Thump, turn to **354**.

83

The officer looks along the line of survivors and says matter-of-factly, 'By my count, there are forty-seven of you left in the qualifying tournament. Lord Carnuss requires that number to be reduced to twelve within the hour. It is time to choose a partner for the next contest, which is called Heavy Metal. Do it now!' If you want to choose the burly Man-Orc on your left, turn to **377**. If you want to choose the bare-chested Barbarian on your right, turn to **234**.

84

When you place the Dragon Balls on the table, the Dragonmaster says in a sombre voice, 'Having only two Dragon Balls means you have a formidable task ahead of you. Follow me.' He walks over to the second iron door in the left-hand wall and unlocks it. He opens the door and beckons you to go through, saying, 'If you survive, knock on the door. I'll be waiting for you.' You draw your sword and walk into a large cave. You hear the door slam shut behind you and hardly have time to think before an enormous bare-chested creature with green skin strides towards you, wielding a massive axe with a double-sided axe head. It has small eyes and long tusks sticking out of its huge mouth. You must fight the ORC CHAMPION.

ORC CHAMPION	SKILL 10	STAMINA 10

If you win, turn to **32**.

85

You begin to panic as the ceiling continues to slide down. Lose 1 LUCK point. If you have a hand axe, turn to **246**. If you have a Vorpal Sword, turn to **28**. If you do not have either of these weapons, turn to **351**.

86

The tunnel continues on until you reach a narrow ravine that descends into the murky depths below. A narrow rope bridge crosses the ravine. If you want to walk across the bridge, turn to **200**. If you want to try jumping across the ravine, turn to **352**.

87

You walk quickly along the tunnel and suddenly catch sight of the Assassin who is drinking from her flask. You call out to her. She turns round and spits out a mouthful of water on the floor. 'Missing me already?' she says smugly, trying not to smile. 'I'm still willing to team up with you, but, seeing as how I saved your skin, I'm going to choose which way we go for the time being. Let's go!' As you walk along, you talk about the Golden Orb, wondering if you have already gone past it or whether it was still to be found up ahead. Turn to **65**.

88

You are breathing hard after the fight, and the acrid smell in the tunnel is making you feel sick. You wade knee-deep through the foul-smelling sewage water over to the stone steps. There is a hole in the wall next to the door. You peer into it but can't see anything. If you want to put your hand into the hole, turn to **305**. If you would rather open the door, turn to **27**.

89

You look round to see that the Monk has dealt with the second Troll, which lies sprawled out on the floor. There is blood seeping through the sleeve of the Monk's left arm, but he tells you that it's just a scratch. A search of the Trolls' clothing yields 4 Gold Pieces, which you share between you. You carry on walking west to where the passageway makes a sharp turn to the right. You continue north for a short distance until the Monk suddenly stops and holds up his hand. 'Wait. I think we are being followed,' he whispers, glancing behind him. 'You walk on so they can hear your footsteps, and I'll hide in the shadows here and ambush whoever it is.' Turn to **373**.

90

You insert the key in the lock and turn it slowly, and are relieved to hear it unlock. The Dragonmaster claps his hands slowly three times and says, 'Now you must select the key to open the third lock.' If you know which key to use, turn to the paragraph with the same number as the key. If you do not know which key to use, turn to **336**.

91

You walk over to the man whose eyes are ice blue. He looks at you without smiling and says very seriously, 'This is a Craggen Knife. I forged it myself. You will need one if you hope to survive today. I would be willing to sell this one for 2 Gold Pieces if you would like to buy it?' You look at the knife and see that it has an ornate handle and a long wavy blade made of bronze. If you want to buy the knife, turn to **371**. If you want to turn down his offer and catch up with Thump, turn to **12**.

92

You take the striker and hit the gong as hard as you can. A low-pitched sound rings out that is painful to listen to. You cover your ears, but there is no escaping the pain in your head, which will permanently affect your balance. Lose 1 SKILL point. If you want to continue walking north, turn to **138**. If you want to enter the new tunnel, turn to **362**.

93

The Thief looks disappointed that nobody else wants to change places with him, but he shrugs his shoulders as though he doesn't care. He need not have worried. The crowd gasps when Lord Carnuss suddenly pulls down on the iron lever and the slabs fall away. You drop through the hole and tumble head over heels down a dark shaft to land on iron spikes at the bottom of a dark pit. Unable to move and bleeding profusely, you lose consciousness. Your adventure is over.

94

If you want to show the black cat to the Ghost-Witch, turn to **19**. If you would rather ignore the Ghost-Witch and walk past her up the stairs, turn to **160**. If you want to go back down the stairs and turn right at the junction, turn to **265**.

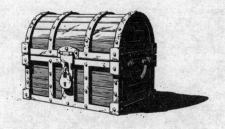

95

The Warrior-Knight has lost his backpack and has nothing on him other than a small leather purse on his belt. You empty the purse and find a ring made of bone and a small bottle labelled 'Potion of Mind Control'. There is a tiny crack in the bottle from where the liquid is seeping out. If you want to put the ring on your finger, turn to **330**. If you want to drink the last drops of liquid in the bottle, turn to **268**. Alternatively, you can continue east (turn to **243**) or turn round and go back to the junction to head west (turn to **80**).

The Zombie lunges forward to grab you with its manacled hands

96

You watch the man break free from his chains and suddenly leap off the page. He lands on the floor and grows quickly into a life-size figure standing opposite you. With green bile spilling out of his broken mouth, he utters a sickly gurgling sound from the back of his throat and lunges forward to grab you with his manacled hands. The spell has released the undead! Lose 1 LUCK point. You are being attacked by a flesh-eating ZOMBIE, and you must defend yourself!

ZOMBIE   *SKILL* 7   *STAMINA* 7

If you win, turn to **338**.

97

The heavy door isn't locked. It opens with a loud creak, and you enter a large room with stone walls and a high ceiling. The room is completely empty except for the headless SKELETON of a large-boned humanoid creature standing at the back of the room. It has plate-steel shoulder pads with spikes protruding from them like the gauntlets, and a silver armband on its left arm. As you walk towards the Skeleton, the door slams shut behind you, and the ceiling starts to slide slowly down the walls, with the sound of stone grinding against stone filling the room. Within seconds, the ceiling is less than three metres above the floor.

You run to the door but it is firmly locked. If you are carrying an Orc skull, turn to **218**. If you do not have a skull in your backpack, turn to **85**.

98

You stand opposite the Thief, who looks dismissively at you and spits on the ground. The gates open and an ox-drawn cart piled high with large iron balls rolls slowly into the arena. The officer instructs everybody to take an iron ball from the cart and stand holding it above their head opposite their partner. The ball is very heavy, and you have difficulty in lifting it up. The Thief also struggles to lift his iron ball above his head. Your arms soon start to shake under the weight of the ball. The crowd cheers as balls begin to drop on to the ground all around the arena with a dull thud, and the eliminated contestants are led away by the guards. The muscles in your arms start to burn and you wonder how much longer you can last. Lose 2 STAMINA points. You glare at the Thief whose face is dripping with sweat. Roll two dice. If the total is higher than the Thief's SKILL score of 5, turn to **267**. If the total is 5 or less, turn to **166**.

99

You uncork the bottle and watch white smoke seep out and swirl round the tunnel. The smoke begins to form itself into a humanoid shape with an evil ghostly face. It is a WILL-O'-THE-WISP. It spins round you several times before flying off east down the tunnel. When it has gone, you discover that everything made of glass you possess has turned to dust, rendering the items useless. Lose 1 LUCK point. If you want carry on east, turn to **201**. If you want to go back and join the Monk, turn to **271**.

100

One of the iron bars is loose, and you are able to prise it away from the wall with your sword. The Mouseling jumps up and down excitedly before pointing to himself and then the floor, signalling that he wants you to lift him down. If you want to do as he asks, turn to **183**. If you want to leave him where he is in the alcove and walk on, turn to **25**.

101

The tunnel leads to a steep flight of steps, going up, which end at a trapdoor. You push the trapdoor up, relieved that it isn't locked. You climb up into a small room that appears to be a storage room full of old furniture covered with a thick layer of dust. There is a door on the right-hand wall with a key in the lock. If you want to open the furniture drawers, turn to **397**. If you want to open the door, turn to **82**.

102

The Man-Orc digs his heels in, shouting at the top of his voice. You stop sliding forward, which gives the Barbarian the chance to take up his position on the rope again. The contest is now deadlocked with neither team able to pull the other forward. The Priestess suddenly lets go of the rope with one hand and points to the sky. A green flash sparks from her ring finger, and the rope suddenly feels easier to pull, as though an invisible hand is helping you pull it. You start to inch your way backwards, and all the wailing and grunting coming from your opponents cannot stop them from being pulled forward. The officer raises his sword when you have dragged them forward by a metre. The stone floor gives way beneath them, and you watch them fall into the void, screaming in terror. Turn to **213**.

103

You place the Gold Piece in the palm of the left hand and watch it close into a clenched fist. At the same time, the right fist opens to allow you to take the scroll. You unroll the parchment and see a short rhyme written on it in black ink.

Note the degrees
Of the Compass Keys
To open the Dragonmaster's door
North is first
Then East and West,
South is number four

You stuff the scroll into your backpack and check the walls for hidden doors and secret passages, but find nothing. You realize your only choice is to walk back to the last junction and head west. As you turn the corner, you don't notice a small panel in the ceiling drop down. Nor do you see the blowpipe appear that is aimed at you. *Test Your Luck*. If you are Lucky, turn to **136**. If you are Unlucky, turn to **315**.

104

You arrive at a doorway in the right-hand wall of the tunnel. You notice that there is a peephole in the middle of the wooden door. If you want to slide it open, turn to **370**. If you want to open the door, turn to **50**. If you want to keep on walking, turn to **236**.

105

The Gatekeeper looks momentarily surprised as you draw your sword. He frowns and points his ring finger at you, whereupon a jagged bolt of lightning slams into your chest. 'Fools and their fortunes are soon parted,' you hear him say as you lose consciousness. You wake up some time later to find yourself in the bowels of a ship bound for the mainland. Your adventure is over.

106

The Hobgoblin catches the key through the bars and lets out a whoop of joy. He unlocks the door and jumps down from the cage, still holding the bell. 'Carnuss's guards saying me dungeon people is freeing me. Not true. Not good. Thinking me never escape! Me free and telling you stairs climbing,' he says, pointing over his shoulder to the staircase with his thumb. He starts walking towards the tunnel you came from, but suddenly stops and looks back at you. 'Me forgetting little man with red hair, green pants. You meet, you ring this,' he says, ringing the bell. 'Him Juggler Jak. Him saying friend, but him not. Him thief. If him seeing, you ringing bell. Him hating bell.' The Hobgoblin places his hands over his ears and pretends to scream. 'Mine 1 Gold Piece. You buy cheap, cheap.' If you want to buy the brass bell, turn to **17**. If you want to decline his offer and walk over to the archways, turn to **393**. If you want to attack the Hobgoblin, turn to **227**.

107

When you place the Dragon Balls on the table, the Dragonmaster says in a sombre voice, 'Finding four Dragon Balls is impressive, but you still have a tough task ahead of you. Follow me.' He walks over to the second iron door in the right-hand wall and unlocks it. He opens the door and beckons you to go through, saying, 'If you survive, knock on the door. I'll be waiting for you.' You draw your sword and walk into a large, musty-smelling cave. You hear the door slam shut behind you and are immediately confronted by an ugly creature with a muscular body, long arms and long fingers that end in sharp claws. It has long curved tusks protruding from its drooling mouth. The CAVE TROLL sniffs the air and strides towards you, wielding a heavy wooden club. You must fight it.

CAVE TROLL   *SKILL* 7   *STAMINA* 8

If you win, turn to **32**.

108

As you slide the panel open, a mouse runs across your feet. You instinctively look down and avoid being blinded by the deadly rays of light coming from the sunstone. You slam the peephole shut, realizing it was a trap. If you want to open the door, turn to **50**. If you want to keep on walking, turn to **236**.

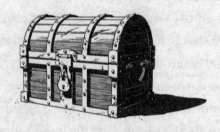

109

The Gnome looks very pleased when you tell him you are going to try to unlock the manacle binding his ankle. 'You'll need an iron key for the manacle. Any iron key will do. They are all the same down here,' he says excitedly. If you have an iron key, turn to **332**. If you do not have an iron key, turn to **76**.

110

You scramble up the ladder and are very relieved to find that the door isn't locked. It opens into a dimly lit tunnel running left and right, which has rough stone walls, hewn out of the rock long ago by Carnuss's slaves. The air is cool and dank, and there is an eerie silence save for the occasional clang of a bell coming from a long way off. You peer into the gloom and decide which way to go. If you want to head west, turn to **7**. If you want to head east in the direction of the sound of the bell, turn to **328**.

111

You tap the silver ring several times and watch an ice storm erupt from it, covering the Lava Demon with a thick blanket of ice. You keep tapping to keep the ice storm flowing until the ring turns black, its magic spent. The cave fills with steam as the ice begins to melt. You seize your chance and run as fast as you can round the pathway to the far side of the fire pit into the new tunnel before the Demon can free itself. Turn to **129**.

A man is sitting on a bench juggling three glass balls

112

There is a T-junction up ahead where you see somebody sitting on a sturdy wooden bench, juggling three small glass balls. He's no more than a metre tall and has curly ginger hair. He is wearing a green cloak over a baggy shirt and pants. When he sees you, he catches the glass balls and jumps off the bench. 'Greetings! I'm Jak the jolly Juggler. You must be one of the contestants,' he says warmly. 'You look in need of a rest. Why don't you sit down for a while on this magic bench? It will revive you. It revived me.' If you want to sit down on the bench, turn to **390**. If you want to attack the Juggler, turn to **319**. If you have a brass bell, turn to **235**.

113

You hear a satisfying click as the key turns in the lock. You are almost blinded by a sudden flash as a high-voltage current passes from the key to your body, making you shake uncontrollably in agony. You are unable to let go of the key, and the Dragonmaster simply looks on as you drop to the floor in a smoking heap. Your adventure is over.

114

The Woodcutter gratefully accepts the food (deduct one of your Provisions) and places it on top of the pile of logs. 'I'm looking forward to eating soon, thank you. But, before I can give you the information, I have been ordered to ask you to solve a puzzle. Are you willing to do that?' If you agree, turn to **186**. If you want to attack the Woodcutter, turn to **37**. If you would rather leave the room and carry on walking up the corridor, turn to **386**.

115

The tunnel continues on for another twenty metres to where there is a stairway going down. You hear clanky footsteps and see an armoured SKELETON appear on the steps. When it nears the top, you see that it is dragging a huge glowing sword behind it and is struggling with the weight of it. The sword looks special, and you decide to fight the Skeleton to get it. You rush forward to attack the Skeleton, which looks barely able to lift the sword over its head.

SKELETON   *SKILL* 5   *STAMINA* 6

If you win, turn to **78**.

116

The corridor turns right, and you walk along it without incident until you come to a junction. Looking straight ahead, you see that the corridor carries on for some distance, fading into the darkness. Looking left, you see there is somebody up ahead lying on the floor, propped up against the wall and groaning. He is holding a war hammer on his lap. It's Thump! If you made a bond with Thump, turn to **233**. If you did not make a bond with Thump, turn to **354**.

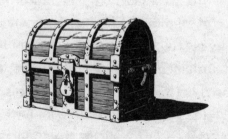

There is an eerie whooshing sound of arrows flying across the arena, many of them hitting their targets. Miraculously, the High Elf's arrow misses you, whistling right past your left ear. There are gasps from the crowd as arrows thud into the contestants, including the arrow lodged in the Elf's shoulder. She pulls it out, cursing that she has been eliminated, and angry that her arrow missed you. Listening to the groans of the injured contestants, you are relieved to have survived. You scan the survivors and see Thump standing, hands on hips, with a big grin on his face. The trumpet blasts out again and the officer instructs the remaining contestants to line up against the wall opposite him while the injured are led out and the dead are dragged from the arena. You walk over to Thump and ask him what happened. 'I never learned how to use a bow and arrow so I figured that if I aimed to miss the Thug, I would be more likely to hit him. And I did!' he says, roaring with laughter. The officer looks along the line of contestants and says without any emotion in his voice, 'By my count, there are forty-eight contestants left in the tournament. Lord Carnuss requires that number to be reduced to twelve within the hour. It is time to choose a partner for the next contest. Do it now!' You agree with Thump's suggestion to split up, at least for now. If you want to choose the Thief on your left, turn to **98**. If you want to choose the Ninja on your right, turn to **184**.

118

You are paralysed by fear and unable to stop yourself from shaking uncontrollably. You try to focus your mind as the Howling Demon bears down on you to rip you apart with its four clawed hands in a frenzied attack. You draw your sword with trembling hands to defend yourself. Reduce your Attack Strength by 4 (or by 2 if you are wielding a Vorpal Sword) during each Attack Round for this battle only.

HOWLING DEMON　　　　*SKILL* 12　　　*STAMINA* 10

If you win, turn to **367**.

119

You jump down into the pit and find yourself knee-deep in Cockroaches. The smell is disgusting. The Cockroaches crawl all over you, but you get to the other side of the pit safely. You are about to climb out when your foot strikes something solid. If you want to plunge your hand into the Cockroaches to find out what it is, turn to **146**. If you want to climb out of the pit immediately, turn to **262**.

120

You manage to get both hands on the handrail, but, as you start to haul yourself up, you see RATS scurrying towards you along the rope. Some start to gnaw on your fingers, and others crawl down your arms and begin gnawing on your face. You try to shake them off, but more and more just keep coming. With virtually no flesh left on your fingers, you do not have the strength to hold on any longer. You fall headlong into the ravine and land on a bed of rocks thirty metres below. Your adventure is over.

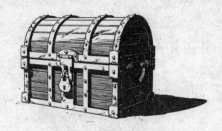

121

You are roused from your deep slumber by somebody poking you in the ribs with the end of a spear. It's another TROLL GUARD. 'Wake up!' he grunts. 'I want you see who is about to slay you.' If you possess a dagger, turn to **13**. If you do not have a dagger, turn to **346**.

122

The box isn't locked, and inside you find some rusty nails and a copper ring. You throw away the nails and examine the ring. There are mysterious runes etched round the inside. If you want to put the ring on your finger, turn to **383**. If you want to put the ring back in the box and open the iron door opposite, turn to **251**.

123

The corridor continues west for fifty metres before turning sharply to the right. You head north and soon arrive at a doorway in the right-hand wall. If you want to open the door, turn to **172**. If you want to carry on walking, turn to **116**.

124

The tunnel finally comes to an end at a T-junction. There is a drawing on the wall in white chalk of a treasure chest and an arrow above it pointing east. Suddenly you hear high-pitched laughter coming from the left-hand tunnel. If you want to turn left and head west, turn to **181**. If you want to turn right and head east, turn to **340**.

125

With your sword held tightly, you stoop down and pass through the archway. Aware of being ambushed at any moment, you walk along the tunnel, ever alert, and see it turn left ahead. You peer round the corner, and, seeing nobody, you head north and walk on for fifty metres to where the tunnel comes to a dead end. There are two huge white clay hands with black-painted fingernails attached to the end wall. The left one is held out with its palm open, and the right one is a clenched fist holding a scroll. There is a sign on the wall, written in what looks like dried blood, which says, 'Pay 1 Gold Piece, no less, no more, to learn the secret of the Dragonmaster's door.' If you want to place 1 Gold Piece in the palm of the open hand, turn to **103**. If you want to try to pull the scroll out of the clenched fist, turn to **306**.

126

Keeping an eye on the statue, you reach down and pick up the ring. It feels ice-cold in your hand. If you want to put it on your finger, turn to **144**. If you would rather put the ring back on the floor and leave the room to walk up the corridor, turn to **331**. Alternatively, if you haven't done so already, you can look in the mirror. Turn to **358**.

127

The door swings open, and you find yourself in another narrow passageway. You hear the door close behind you, and you walk on until you come to another bronze door at the end of the passageway where you see a man wearing a dark blue coif cap and long robes sitting on a chair with his arms folded. When he sees you, he stands up and rubs his chin, and you notice that he has a large gemstone ring on his forefinger. 'Well, I never,' he says in a calm voice. 'Nobody was meant to survive this dungeon. But here you are. I presume you have the Golden Orb in your possession. I am the Gatekeeper, and I am obliged to authenticate the Orb before I can open the final door.' If you want to show the Orb to the Gatekeeper, turn to **206**. If you want to attack him, turn to **105**.

128

The Ghost-Witch smiles contentedly and says, 'That is wonderful. I am so happy that you found my little Lawrence. Please put him on my tray.' If you want to give the cat to the Ghost-Witch, turn to **221**. If you would rather keep the cat and walk past the Ghost-Witch, turn to **160**.

There is a white marble statue of Lord Carnuss sitting on a throne

129

You walk north along the tunnel for what seems like ages until it finally comes to an end at a magnificent gold door covered with intricate etchings of fire-breathing dragons. The Golden Dragon door isn't locked and opens into an opulent chamber that has a white marble floor and plush furnishings bedecked with statuettes, vases, inlaid boxes and ornaments. But what interests you the most is the white marble statue of Lord Carnuss sitting on a grand throne set against the far wall. He is holding a Golden Orb in his lap. If you want to examine the throne, turn to **36**. If you want to search the chamber, turn to **343**.

130

Thump counts the raised hands and says, 'That's seven in favour of the Priestess and five in favour of the Man-Orc. The Priestess will be our anchor.' Everybody takes up their position on the rope with the Barbarian at the front, with you and Thump in second and third position, and the Priestess at the back. You watch the opposing team take their positions on the rope with a Berserker at the front and a giant of a Warrior at the back as their anchor. Gripping the rope tightly, everybody leans back to take up the strain. The officer raises his sword and shouts, 'When I say heave, pull on the rope as hard as you can! The first team to drag the other team forward by a metre will be judged the winner. Get ready! One, two, three – heave!'

Sweating profusely in the heat, but encouraged by the grimacing faces of your opponents, you lean as far back as you can, pulling on the rope with all your might. The minutes pass, with neither team able to pull the other forward, when suddenly the Priestess lets go of the rope and points to the sky. A green flash sparks from her ring finger, and the rope suddenly feels easier to pull, as though an invisible hand is helping you pull it. You start to inch your way backwards, and all the wailing and grunting coming from your opponents cannot stop them from being pulled forward. The officer raises his sword when you have dragged them forward by a metre. The stone floor gives way beneath them, and you watch them fall into the void, screaming in terror. Turn to **213**.

131

You jump to one side, but are hit by two arrows, one in the arm and one in the shoulder. Lose 4 STAMINA points. If you are still alive, turn to **317**.

132

You check the box for traps, and, satisfied there isn't one, you slowly lift the lid. Inside, you find a silver key lying on top of a blue silk cushion. Add 1 LUCK point. You take the key and await your next instruction, but the room remains silent. If you want to open another box, turn to **388**. If you want to open the door, turn to **165**.

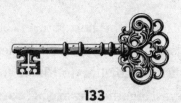

133

After changing places with him, Fingers looks at you with a smug smile on his face. 'One thing I've learned during my years as a thief,' he says, grinning, 'is how to detect traps!' The crowd gasps when Carnuss suddenly pulls down on the iron lever and the slabs fall away. You drop down the hole and tumble head over heels down a dark shaft to land on iron spikes at the bottom of a dark pit. Unable to move and bleeding profusely, you lose consciousness. Your adventure is over.

134

You climb out of the water and find Bloodworms inside your clothing that are sucking your blood. You manage to pull them all off, but they leave deep red marks on your skin that are painful to the touch. Lose 2 STAMINA points. You climb the steps to the new tunnel and head north. Turn to **147**.

135

The chest isn't locked. You lift the lid and are immediately enveloped by a dense cloud of tiny MOZFLIES with their ultra-fast-beating wings making a loud buzzing noise. You swat them with your hands, but they get in your mouth, your nose, your eyes, your ears, your hair and even inside your clothing. The attack does not last long, and the Mozflies fly off down the tunnel in search of new prey. You are covered in bites and begin to itch terribly all over. If you possess a small bottle of Mullweed Oil, turn to **54**. If you do not have Mullweed Oil, turn to **318**.

136

A small dart is fired at you by an unseen assailant, but it flies past your head. You hear it hit the floor and run off down the tunnel, not stopping until you reach the stone archway. If you left your sword in the wooden box, turn to **252**. If you are still carrying your sword, turn to **71**.

137

While holding the door handle, a small poisonous SPIDER hidden in a crevice above the door drops down on its silk thread on to the back of your hand. But, before it has chance to bite you, you flick it off your hand and watch it scurry away into the gloom. Unable to open the iron door, you have no choice but to turn round and walk back in the direction of the sound of the bell. Turn to **328**.

138

Ahead, you see a wooden box that is fixed to the left-hand wall. It has a hinged lid with a coin engraved on it. There are some words below the coin, which read: 'Heads for a Purse, Tails for a Curse'. You lift the lid up and find a shiny copper coin inside the box. If you want to toss the coin in the air, turn to **258**. If you want to keep on walking, turn to **348**.

139

Picking a passage through the candles, you walk over to the shelf and see that the helmet is finely crafted and has a full face guard. If you want to try the helmet on for size, turn to **210**. If you want to put it back on the shelf, and if you have not done so already, you can examine the shield (turn to **325**) or, if you want to leave the room and continue walking up the tunnel, turn to **86**.

140

If you are wearing a bone ring, turn to **199**. If you are not wearing this ring, turn to **182**.

The spectators are finally allowed into the arena late in the afternoon. They cheer the contestants, some of whom look as though they are about to pass out from heat exhaustion. By the time the arena is full, ten contestants are lying face down in the sand. A trumpet fanfare blasts out to signal the arrival of Lord Carnuss. The spectators stand to applaud him as he takes his place on his ornate throne while the unconscious contestants are dragged out of the arena, their contest over before it has even begun. Carnuss raises his arms to silence the trumpet and acknowledge the crowd. Standing next to Carnuss is a tall, mean-faced officer in a red uniform who steps forward to address the contestants with his sword raised in the air. 'Thank you for your patience,' he says insincerely. 'You may now drink water.' You do so eagerly – add 1 STAMINA point. 'As you have been informed by Lord Carnuss, only twelve of you will enter the Dungeon of Despair. Ten contestants have been eliminated already, and another ninety-eight are about to be eliminated in a qualifying tournament. The first round is called Bull's Eye, and you will need a partner for this contest. Choose one now!' With no information to go on, you look at the people closest to you. If you want to team up with Thump, turn to **291**. If you want to choose the High Elf, turn to **47**. If you want to choose the Pirate, turn to **361**.

142

You place your Provisions on the table (make a note on your *Adventure Sheet*) and watch the Dragonmaster put his hands behind his back. He waits a few seconds before saying, 'I am holding a die in one of my hands. You must guess which hand it is in. Guess correctly and you can play the game. Guess wrongly and it's game over for you.' If you want to choose his left hand, turn to **341**. If you want to choose his right hand, turn to **205**.

143

You are infected by the Ghoul's toxic blood. You feel your limbs stiffen, making it difficult to wield your sword. Your body goes numb, and you are unable to move. You remain conscious, but are completely paralysed. The Ghoul licks its festering lips in anticipation of its next meal. You are about to be eaten alive. Your adventure is over.

144

You notice the number 111 etched on the inside of the ring as you slide it on to your middle finger. The statue's eyes flick open, and in a low voice it hisses a chilling warning. 'They who steal the Ring of Ice, my sword will cut and chop and slice!' The Warrior statue stands up, draws its sword and steps down from its plinth to attack you. If you want to fight the BRONZE WARRIOR, turn to **231**. You may Escape, but you must lose 2 STAMINA points as the Warrior will wound you as you flee. Turn to **331**.

145

The corridor soon comes to a dead end. There is a trapdoor against the wall that lifts up to reveal a dark, spiral-shaped chute. If you want to slide down the chute, turn to **320**. If you want to walk back to the cavern, turn to **169**.

146

You reach down and touch what feels like a large iron ring handle. You pull the handle and lift up a trapdoor with Cockroaches running up your arm and watch thousands of the hissing insects disappear down a shaft. You peer down the shaft and see that it gives access to a tunnel below heading north. If you want to slide down the shaft into the new tunnel, turn to **329**. If you want to climb out of the pit, turn to **262**.

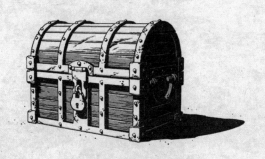

A giant horned creature rises up from the lava belching fire

147

The tunnel has a gentle incline, and you feel the air getting noticeably hotter. The tunnel leads into a large cave that is a bubbling cauldron of molten lava. You see that there is a narrow stone pathway running round the edge of the fire pit along the left-hand wall to another tunnel entrance. As soon as you set foot on the pathway, a giant horned creature enveloped in flames and belching fire rises slowly up from the lava with smoke escaping from the many fissures on its torso. It is a LAVA DEMON, a malevolent creature made of molten rock. It reaches down to scoop up a handful of lava to hurl at you. If you are wearing a Ring of Ice, turn to the number that is etched on the inside of the ring. If you do not have this ring, turn to **296**.

148

The Dragonmaster remains silent for a few moments before saying in a stern voice, 'That is a grave error on your part. You have failed in your quest, but, thanks to the generosity of the great Lord Carnuss, your life will be spared for being the first contestant to get to this point.' The Dragonmaster pushes a lever down on the wall behind him, which opens a trapdoor in the floor above a chute. He tells you to slide down the chute, adding, 'Freedom awaits you.' If you want to slide down the chute, turn to **214**. If you want to attack the Dragonmaster, turn to **38**.

149

You see your opponent shaking under the weight of the iron ball, but you are shaking too, with the burning pain in your arms almost unbearable. Turn to **166**.

150

The Gatekeeper shakes his head and says, 'Not knowing his age is disrespectful to Lord Carnuss. That means you cannot win the Orb. I will open the door and you must leave here now without the Orb.' If you want to accept the Gatekeeper's ruling, turn to **326**. If you want to attack the Gatekeeper, turn to **105**.

151

You find a gold key on a chain around the Cyclops' neck with the number 270 stamped on it. You put the key in your pocket and search the chamber. Finding nothing else of interest, you think about which way to go. If you want to leave the room and head north, turn to **230**.If you want to leave the room and go back down the staircase and turn right at the junction, turn to **265**.

152

You begin turning the pages and soon realize that it is a book about the construction of Lord Carnuss's dungeon. There are mentions of 'locks' in the bowels of the dungeon, and warnings about Dragons and Demons. Puzzled and wanting to learn more, you skip to the back of the book where you find floor plans of the dungeon. You recognize the entrance and the tunnel, staircase and corridor that led you to the library. On the next page, you see that the east corridor you are in turns north and ends at what looks like a chute down to a tunnel. The following page shows that the north end of this tunnel has two rooms off it before coming to a rope bridge over a ravine. The tunnel continues north, with another room off it, before ending at a T-junction. The rooms on the left side of the tunnel are marked Candle Room and Spider Pit Room. The room on the right side is marked Firewood Room. You turn the page, but, much to your annoyance, the remaining pages have been ripped out of the book. You put it back on the shelf and decide what to do. If you have not done so already, you can either open the book entitled *Mages and Magic* (turn to **263**) or open the book entitled *Dead and Undead* (turn to **248**). If you want to leave the library and continue up the corridor, turn to **179**.

153

You jump on to the rope and slide down it until you reach the tunnel entrance. You suddenly feel a sharp pain in your leg where you have been hit by a small object. Blood starts to trickle down your leg. Lose 1 STAMINA point. You look in the tunnel and see the Troglodyte loading a stone into his slingshot. You push back against the wall and swing on the rope, aiming to dive feet first into the tunnel. Roll two dice. If the total is equal to or less than your SKILL score, turn to **188**. If the number is greater than your SKILL score, turn to **256**.

154

You walk on for some distance and see a small man with a long grey beard sitting cross-legged on the floor, leaning back against the tunnel wall. As you get closer, you see that he is a GNOME and that he is chained to the wall by his ankle. There is a sign fixed to the wall above his head that says 'Free Food'. You ask him what the free food is, and he replies, 'Me. I am the free food. I've been left out here for the Raptorex to eat. One of the Troll Guards put up that sign. It's not funny.' If you want to try to free the Gnome, turn to **109**. If you want to leave him and walk on, turn to **247**.

The arrow fired by Thump flies over your head, missing you by some distance. The crowd gasps as the contestants fall to the ground, groaning, clutching the arrows lodged in their torsos. The trumpet sounds again, and the officer instructs the remaining contestants to line up against the far wall while the injured are led out and the dead are dragged from the arena. You walk over to Thump and ask him why he aimed at you. 'I was never taught how to use a bow and arrow so I figured that if I aimed it at you, I would be bound to miss!' he says, roaring with laughter. You tell him that having seen him aim at you, you aimed at him, but missed. 'That's not funny,' he says, frowning. 'Let's not risk fighting each other again. We should split up for the next contest.' The officer looks along the line of contestants and says coldly, 'By my count, there are forty-eight contestants left in the tournament. Lord Carnuss requires that number to be reduced to twelve within the hour. It is time to choose a partner for the next contest, which is called Heavy Metal. Do it now!' If you want to choose the Thief on your left, turn to **98**. If you want to choose the Ninja on your right, turn to **184**.

156

The Ghost-Witch's eyes light up and she closes in on you, almost touching your nose with hers. 'Where is he?' she asks excitedly in a soft, breathy voice. If you possess a small cat made of black marble, turn to **94**. If you want to tell the Ghost-Witch that you do not know where the cat is, turn to **297**.

157

As you are pulled towards the Bloodbeast, you become aware of a noxious smell of gas coming from its lair that makes you feel dizzy and light-headed. You struggle to draw your sword with your free hand, but pass out, unaware of being dragged into the pool of toxic slime inside the Bloodbeast's lair. Once the slime has softened you up, the Bloodbeast will feast on your flesh. Your adventure is over.

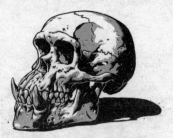

158

Ahead, you see a wooden door in the right-hand wall from which you hear the sound of somebody chopping wood. If you want to open the door, turn to **72**. If you want to carry on walking up the corridor, turn to **386**.

159

You shake the Assassin's hand, telling her that you wouldn't normally form an alliance with an Assassin, but this dungeon isn't normal. You see the faintest of smiles on her face before she turns and strides off up the tunnel. You catch up with her and talk about the Golden Orb, wondering if you have already gone past it or whether it was still to be found up ahead. You are deep in discussion when you come to a new passageway in the right-hand wall. 'Seeing as how I just saved your skin, I'm going to choose which way we go for the time being,' she says forcefully. 'We are going to head north!' You turn right and soon arrive at the entrance to a narrow tunnel in the right-hand wall that has a rough stone floor sloping downwards into darkness. 'I don't like the look of that tunnel. Let's keep going north,' she says without stopping. Turn to **65**.

160

The Ghost-Witch's eyes widen, and she lets out a high-pitched screech that echoes down the passageway. She glides down the staircase and reaches out with a bony hand that passes through you as though you are a ghost yourself. You feel a sudden chill, and a sensation like an ice-cold hand squeezing your heart. Lose 1 SKILL point and 5 STAMINA points. If you are still alive, you watch the Ghost-Witch glide down the passageway and disappear left round the corner. If you want to climb to the top of the staircase, turn to **327**. If you want to go back down the steps and turn right at the junction, turn to **265**.

161

The Hobgoblin points to his left and says, 'Key! Look! There!' You walk to the back of the cavern, turn over a large stone and find a brass key underneath it. 'Throw to me! Quick!' the Hobgoblin shouts impatiently. If you want to throw the key up to Hobgoblin, turn to **106**. If you would rather keep the key and walk on, turn to **393**.

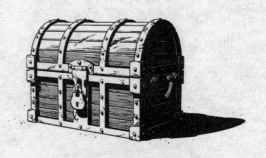

The door bursts open on to a multi-eyed creature with spiked teeth

162

You unlock the door and turn the handle. The door bursts open and you are immediately struck by a giant tongue that whips out from a huge mouth lined with the long, spiked teeth of a multi-eyed creature. Its head is pressed hard against the door frame, filling it completely. You are staring into the slavering mouth of a terrifying BLOODBEAST! Roll two dice. If the total is equal to or less than your SKILL score, turn to **220**. If the number is greater than your SKILL score, turn to **289**.

163

Your sight gradually returns but not quite fully. Everything you see around you is slightly out of focus. Lose 1 SKILL point. You rummage through the Ratmen's pockets and find a piece of chalk, a glass eyeball, a small bottle labelled Weezle Juice, a small cat carved out of black marble and a chewed bone. After taking what you want, you set off again. Turn to **236**.

164

The Imp looks a little apprehensive when you draw your sword. He quickly turns and dashes over to his Spikle. He picks it up and steps inside the wheel. 'What luck. It's not damaged at all,' he says smugly. He scoots off and disappears round the bend, heading east. 'I'll get you again on the way back, wormbrain!' he shouts and starts laughing hysterically. The laughter soon dies away, and you set off again, now heading north. Turn to **104**.

165

You reach the door and place the key in the lock only to find that the door isn't locked after all. You leave the room to head west along the tunnel. Turn to **198**.

166

You begin to lose your grip on the iron ball and, much to the delight of your opponent and the cheering crowd, there is nothing you can do but let it drop to the ground. A guard grabs your arm and leads you out of the arena. You can't believe that you are out of the contest so soon. Your adventure is over.

167

The old man pockets the Gold Piece and hands you a tarnished white-gold signet ring that has a sword etched on its face. 'Go on, put it on,' he urges. You slide it on to your little finger and suddenly feel extra alert. It is a Ring of Dexterity that will improve your combat skills. Add 1 SKILL point and 1 LUCK point. You thank the old man and leave the room, turning left to open the door at the end of the corridor. Turn to **309**.

168

The bread is stale but edible, and the cheese tastes sour even after cutting off the mould. But you are hungry and devour everything on the plate, washing it down with slugs of water. Add 2 STAMINA points. If you have not done so already, you can either open the chest (turn to **385**) or try to open the door at the back of the room (turn to **67**). If you would rather leave the room and head north up the passageway, turn to **230**. If you want to leave the room and run back down the staircase and turn right at the junction, turn to **265**.

169

You hurry back along the corridor, passing two doors until you reach the staircase. You hear murmuring voices and the sound of footsteps in the stairwell. If you want to draw your sword and face whoever is coming up the staircase, turn to **364**. If you want to run back down the corridor and slide down the chute, turn to **320**.

170

The Dragonmaster watches you place your charms on the table and says, 'For each charm you give me, I will let you add 1 to your dice roll total. The game will now begin.' You roll your dice at the same time as the Dragonmaster rolls his three dice. The total of his three dice is 9. If the total of your dice and bonus is 9 or less, turn to **55**. If the total is 10 or greater, turn to **357**.

171

You reach down to pick up the object, which you discover is a glass jar containing 2 Gold Pieces. You decide to climb up the ladder before any more Snakes strike you. Turn to **110**.

172

The door isn't locked and opens into a storeroom with shelves stacked with dungeon equipment. The floor is crammed with barrels and boxes, and at the back of the room there is a portly man in a white apron sitting on a chair with his legs up on the counter, fast asleep and snoring loudly. If you want to wake the Storeman, turn to **23**. If you want to close the door and carry on walking up the corridor, turn to **116**.

173

The narrow passageway continues north, and you soon arrive at a solid oak door in the left-hand wall. You listen at the door but hear nothing. If you want to open the door, turn to **97**. If you want to continue walking, turn to **249**.

174

You pass by a water fountain in the left-hand wall. It is in the shape of large fish head from which water is gushing out of its mouth into a stone bowl. If you want to drink at the fountain, turn to **302**. If you want to press on, turn to **365**.

175

The Dragonmaster taps his fingers on the table and says disdainfully, 'Four Compass Keys are needed for this test. No more, no less. It is unfortunate that you failed to find them, but that is what Lord Carnuss expected, of course.' Turn to **336**.

176

You stand on the slab and watch the Monk stand on slab 2 and finally the Thief, who steps cautiously on to slab 5. Your heart begins to pound in your chest when Lord Carnuss reaches for an iron lever protruding from the wall of the cave entrance. The crowd goes silent when he takes hold of it with both hands. 'Contestants, you are about to enter my Dungeon of Despair. When I pull down on this lever, you will drop through the floor. I should warn you that one of you will not survive the fall! If any of you want to change places with another contestant, do so now!' The Thief raises his hand and says, 'I'll swap if anybody else will?' If you want to change places with Fingers, turn to **133**. If you want to stay where you are, turn to **342**.

177

The statuettes are of demons and dragons, and the vases all contain bunches of long-stemmed black roses. The ornaments are of no use to you, but you open a small black-lacquered box on a side table and find a gold signet ring engraved with a dragon's head. If you want to put the ring on your finger, turn to **211**. If you would rather put the ring back in the box and walk over to the throne to pick up the Orb, turn to **228**.

178

You head west with the Monk, exchanging stories about the dangers you have faced in the dungeon. 'The Goblins were easy to defeat,' he says boastfully, 'but I was nearly eaten by a Raptorex. I had to hide in an alcove while it rampaged through the tunnel. But I did manage to squeeze some information out of one of the Troll Guards I gave a bit of a clobbering to before leaving him to rot in a cell. He agreed it was better than me leaving him chained to the wall for the Raptorex to find. He told me that you need special keys to escape from the dungeon. They are the four gold Compass Keys. Each one has a number stamped on it that represents the cardinal points on a compass. The north key has 360 stamped on it, the south key has 180 stamped on it and so on. Have you found any?' Before you can answer, you see two tall, stocky figures in leather armour running towards you, wielding long spears. They have green warty skin and huge tusked mouths. They are TROLL GUARDS. 'These Guards are beginning to annoy me,' says Uzman, sounding a bit bored. 'You take the one on the left, and I'll deal with the one on the right.'

TROLL GUARD   *SKILL* 9   *STAMINA* 9

If you win, turn to **89**.

179

You follow the corridor east until it turns left and heads north. Around the corner you see the body of a Troll Guard propped up against the left-hand wall with a bloodied sword across his lap and a small drawstring bag hanging from his belt. If you want to take the sword, turn to **345**. If you want to take the bag, turn to **24**. If you want to keep on walking, turn to **145**.

A spiked wheel is being ridden by a small green-skinned creature

180

You put the key in the keyhole. The lock is larger than the other locks and it feels like you can turn the key either way. If you want to turn the key clockwise, turn to **113**. If you want to turn the key counterclockwise, turn to **45**.

181

The walls of the roughly hewn rock tunnel become smoother and are interspersed with carvings of dragons and demons. The floor has a layer of sand on it with fresh footprints heading west. The tunnel soon starts to curve slowly round to the right, and, as you continue on, you hear the high-pitched laughter again. Suddenly a large wooden wheel with an iron rim and pyramid-shaped spikes comes hurtling round the bend at high speed. The wheel has footholds on the inside of the rim like a giant treadmill and is being ridden by a small green-skinned creature with a wide mouth, wild eyes, pointed ears and a long ponytail trailing behind him. It's a wicked IMP, and he is laughing manically as he steers his Spikle straight at you! Roll two dice. If the total is equal to or less than your SKILL score, turn to **286**. If the number is greater than your SKILL score, turn to **303**.

182

The toxins in the Demon's saliva soon make you feel very ill. You break out in a fever and stagger down the steps with one hand against the wall to hold yourself up. You begin to sway on your feet and cannot stop yourself from falling flat on your face. Lose 1 SKILL point and 5 STAMINA points. If you are still alive, turn to **39**.

183

You lift the Mouseling down on to the floor, and he immediately runs north up the tunnel, beckoning you to follow him. You only need to walk slowly to keep up with him, and it's not long before he comes to a stop in front of a large hole in the floor. There is a rope suspended from the ceiling that drops down into the hole and disappears into darkness. The Mouseling points at the rope and wags his finger at you with a frown on his furry face. He then turns and vanishes into a hole in the tunnel wall before reappearing, carrying a Gold Piece. He places it on the floor, bows and disappears back into the hole, from where you hear excited high-pitched voices. You put the Gold Piece in your pocket and tug on the rope. It feels like it would support your weight. If you want to slide down the rope, turn to **378**. If you want to walk round the hole and on up the tunnel, turn to **232**.

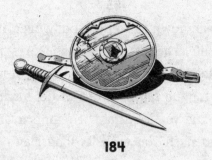

184

You stand opposite the Ninja, who looks at you with piercing eyes, which is all you can see of his masked face. The gates open and an ox-drawn cart piled high with large iron balls rolls slowly into the arena. The officer instructs everybody to take an iron ball from the cart and stand holding it above their head opposite their partner. The iron ball is very heavy, and you have difficulty lifting it. The Ninja shows surprising strength in deftly lifting the iron ball above his head. Your arms soon start to shake under the weight of the ball. The crowd cheers as balls begin to drop on to the ground all around the arena with a dull thud, and the eliminated contestants are led away by the guards. The muscles in your arms start to burn, and you wonder how much longer you can last. Lose 2 STAMINA points. With his arms held rigid in the air, the Ninja shows no sign of buckling under the weight of the ball. Roll two dice. If the total is higher than the Ninja's SKILL score of 6, turn to **22**. If the total is 6 or less, turn to **166**.

185

When you reach down to roll the body over, it suddenly twitches into life. The man sits up and stares at you with wide-open, bloodshot eyes. He has a maggot-ridden face with a black tongue hanging out of his gaping mouth. He stands up and you see that the man is a GHOUL that reaches out to slash you with its long claws. You must fight it!

GHOUL   *SKILL* 8   *STAMINA* 7

If you lose three Attack Rounds, turn to **143**. If you win without losing three Attack Rounds, turn to **255**.

186

The Woodcutter points at the log and says, 'It took me ten minutes to chop this log into two pieces. How long would it have taken me to chop the log into three pieces instead?' If you know the number of minutes, turn to that number. If you do not know the answer, turn to **254**.

187

You search in vain through your backpack for something to kill the Parasites. You begin to feel desperately unwell as the virus spreads through your bloodstream. Angry lumps start appearing all over your body where the infection takes hold, and it's not long before you pass out from the pain, never to recover. Your adventure ends in the darkness in the tunnel.

188

You swing into the tunnel, hitting the Troglodyte with both feet to send him flying. He jumps up, shakes his head and runs off down the tunnel, calling for help. You think about chasing after him, but decide against it since the tunnel roof is very low and would restrict your movement. There is a wooden stool by the entrance with a tin box underneath it. The box contains 2 Gold Pieces and a small solid gold ball with a dragon motif on it. Add 1 LUCK point. You pocket the items and grab hold of the rope and climb out of the well. With nothing else to see in the cavern, you hurry over to the new passageway in case the Troglodyte returns with reinforcements. Turn to **376**.

189

The Snakes are small but slippery-quick, and there at least twenty of them in the pit. They are also poisonous! You must react quickly to avoid being bitten. You draw your sword and attack!

First SNAKE	SKILL 5	STAMINA 3
Second SNAKE	SKILL 4	STAMINA 4
Third SNAKE	SKILL 5	STAMINA 4

Fight the Snakes one at a time. If you defeat all three Snakes, turn to **219**. You may Escape by climbing up the ladder to open the door, but you must lose 2 STAMINA points as one of the other Snakes will bite you as you flee. Turn to **110**.

190

The dagger flies past your head and clatters against the stone wall. You pick it up and slide it into your belt and walk over to the shelf at the back of the room with Azurra Xang screaming angrily at you. 'You'll regret this!' she shouts. 'May the Fireworms of Slann burn through your eyeballs!' Ignoring her angry outburst, you look inside the silver chalice and find a small solid silver ball that is etched with a dragon motif. You place both items in your backpack and leave the room to carry on up the tunnel with the Assassin still cursing you at the top of her voice. Turn to **124**.

191

Three arrows thud into your shield. You look to your left and see that the Assassin has been struck by another arrow, this time in the stomach. It doesn't stop her, and she runs at the Zanth Archers with her spear held high, ready to strike. You charge at the archers who fired their arrows at you, striking the first one down before he has time to fire another arrow at you. You fight the other two one at a time.

First ZANTH ARCHER	SKILL 7	STAMINA 5
Second ZANTH ARCHER	SKILL 7	STAMINA 6

If you win, turn to **382**.

192

You lift the lid and suddenly feel a sharp pain in your wrist. You have triggered a dart trap! Lose 2 STAMINA points and roll one die. If you roll a 6, you must also lose 1 SKILL point. Trying to ignore the pain, you pull the small dart out of your wrist and look inside the box to find a small solid copper ball that is etched with a dragon motif. You put it in your backpack and decide what to do next. If you have not done so already, you can either open the book entitled *Dead and Undead* (turn to **248**) or open the book entitled *Dungeon of Despair* (turn to **152**). If you want to leave the library and continue up the corridor, turn to **179**.

193

The Dragonmaster bangs his fist on the table and points his finger at you. 'Liar! Finding five Dragon Balls is impossible. Dishonesty does not go unpunished!' he shouts loudly. A jagged bolt of lightning flies out from the ring on his finger and slams into your chest. The force of it sends you flying, and you smash your head against the back wall. You slump to the ground and, barely able to move, you can do nothing but watch the Dragonmaster push a lever down on the wall that opens a trapdoor in the floor near to him. He walks over and drags you to the trapdoor and pushes you down into a chute. As you slide down, you hear him shout, 'Be gone with you!' Turn to **214**.

194

You struggle desperately to take the bottle out of your pocket. You are weak from holding your breath, but manage to uncork the bottle and empty out its contents. The acidic Weezle Juice starts to dissolve the Glugg's jelly-like body. It ejects you immediately, trying to rid itself of the acid. Add 1 LUCK point. You stand up and walk on, leaving the decomposing body of the Glugg behind, and soon arrive at a junction. The new tunnel in the left-hand wall is narrow and has a very low ceiling. There is a bad smell of rotten eggs coming from it, and you decide to carry straight on. Turn to **115**.

195

Thump slaps you on the back and shakes your hand firmly. 'By the beard of Bigleg, our bond is built!' he says solemnly with his eyes fixed on yours. 'Now let's find that Orb!' Once outside, the officer leads you along a dusty track that is lined with hundreds of cheering spectators. Walking along, you notice a white-haired old man in the crowd. He is waving at you, trying to get your attention, and when he catches your eye he beckons you over to speak to him. If you want to stop to speak to the old man, turn to **284**. If you want to keep on walking, turn to **12**.

196

The Dwarf screams at the top of his voice and strides towards you with his swords raised in the air. You must fight the angry Dwarf.

DWARF   SKILL *6*   STAMINA *5*

After you win your first Attack Round, turn to **285**.

A small rodent-like creature is trapped behind iron bars

197

You are knocked down and run over by the Spikle. One of its metal spikes pierces your leg as it rolls over you, wounding you badly. Lose 1 SKILL point and 4 STAMINA points. The Imp doesn't stop and carries on riding his Spikle down the corridor. 'I'll get you again on the way back, wormbrain!' he shouts and starts laughing hysterically. The laughter soon dies away, and, after bandaging your leg, you set off north again, limping badly. Turn to **104**.

198

You walk on slowly to where the tunnel turns sharply right. With your sword at the ready, you peer round the corner and see a tiny humanoid creature with a rodent-like head trapped behind iron bars in an alcove in the left-hand wall. It is less than half a metre tall and is wearing a tiny suit of leather armour. It's a MOUSELING, one of the rarely seen creatures who live in small tunnel networks inside caves. When he sees you, he starts squeaking and waving his tiny paws in the air, gesturing for you to free him. If you want to help him escape, turn to **100**. If you want to ignore his plea for help and walk on, turn to **25**.

199

There are toxins in the Demon's saliva, but they have no effect on you. Add 1 LUCK point. Turn to **39**.

200

You step on to the wobbly bridge and walk slowly across. When you reach the middle of the bridge, you step unknowingly into a void. The wooden boards look to be in place, but it's an illusion – three boards are missing! As you begin to fall, you try desperately to grab the rope handrail to save yourself from disappearing through the gap. Roll two dice. If the total rolled is the same or less than your SKILL score, turn to **241**. If the total rolled is greater than your SKILL score, turn to **275**.

201

The tunnel soon comes to a dead end where a rockfall blocks your way. There's a slight draught but no way through. The Monk was right. You are about to turn round and head back when you catch sight of a screwed-up piece of paper in the rubble. There is a note on it that says, 'Do not turn the gold key numbered 180 clockwise in the lock. Turn it counterclockwise.' You sit down on a rock to rest for a while, turning an imaginary key left and right in the air as you ponder the challenges ahead. The short rest is welcome. Add 1 STAMINA point. With your route ahead blocked, you decide to hurry back down the tunnel to catch up with the Monk and head west. Turn to **271**.

202

There is an eerie whooshing sound as the arrows fly across the arena, followed by the sickening thud of many of them hitting their targets. The crowd gasps as contestants fall to the ground, clutching the arrows lodged in their torsos. The arrow you fire at Thump flies past his head and bounces off the wall behind him at the same time as Thump's arrow whistles over your head. You both start grinning, relieved to have survived unscathed. You barely notice the groans of the injured contestants or the noise of the spectators. The trumpet blasts out again and the officer instructs the remaining contestants to line up against the far wall while the injured and the dead are led or dragged out of the arena. Standing next to Thump, you ask him why he aimed his bow at you. 'I never learned how to use a bow and arrow so I thought that if I fired it at you, I would be bound to miss!' he says, roaring with laughter. You tell him that you could have hit him, but decided not to. 'How very considerate of you,' he says with a wry smile. 'Let's not risk fighting each other again. We should split up for the next contest.' The officer looks along the line of contestants and says without any emotion in his voice, 'By my count, there are forty-eight contestants left in the tournament. Lord Carnuss requires that number to be reduced to twelve within the hour. It is time to choose a partner for the next contest, which is called Heavy Metal. Do it now!' If you want to choose the Thief on your left, turn to **98**. If you want to choose the Ninja on your right, turn to **184**.

203

The words form a message that reads, 'To leave the chamber, touch the right eye of the right-hand dragon and the left eye of the left-hand dragon at the same time.' If you want to walk over to the throne to touch the eyes of the dragons, turn to **60**. If you want to pick up the Orb, turn to **228**.

204

The breastplate fits you perfectly and will protect you in combat. Add 1 point to your Attack Strength during combat while wearing the armour. You search the end wall for a secret doorway, but find nothing. You have no option but to walk back down the tunnel to the T-junction. Turn to **33**.

205

The Dragonmaster brings his arm forward and opens his hand to reveal a black die. Add 1 LUCK point. 'You guessed correctly,' he says calmly as he hands you the die. 'You are now equipped to play the game, but the odds are against you winning!' Turn to **324**.

206

You take the Orb out of your backpack and hand it to the Gatekeeper. He holds it close to his face, admiring the workmanship in the dragons. 'Merciful Manticores, it is indeed the Golden Orb,' he exclaims, and lets out a long, low whistle. 'Your final task is to solve a simple puzzle. Answer it correctly, and you are free to go. Answer it incorrectly, and you must forfeit the Orb. Listen carefully. When Baron Sukumvit was twelve years old, Lord Carnuss was half his age. If Baron Sukumvit is now forty-eight years old, how old is Lord Carnuss?' If you know the answer, turn to the paragraph with the same number. If you do not know the answer, turn to **150**. If you want to attack the Gatekeeper, turn to **105**.

207

The tunnel soon veers left and as you walk along you become aware of an acrid smell in the air. Continuing north, you reach a marble urn set against the left-hand wall that is full to the brim with a sharp-smelling dark liquid that makes you gag. If you want to hold your nose and poke your sword around in the urn, turn to **304**. If you would rather walk on, turn to **43**.

208

You grab one of the gauntlets, but it is difficult to keep hold of it as it thrashes around in the air. You are forced to let go of it when the second gauntlet starts clawing at you with its steel-tipped fingers. Lose 2 STAMINA points. Once free, the gauntlets come together and glide over to the door and start scratching at it manically. The door suddenly opens on its own, and the gauntlets immediately turn and go back down the tunnel. You seize your chance and slip through the open door. Turn to **173**.

209

While catching your breath, you take the gold key that is hanging on a string cord around the Monk's neck. You see that it has the number 360 stamped on it. You put it in your pocket, together with 2 Gold Pieces from the leather purse on his belt. You also find a gold envelope inside his tunic containing a handwritten note that reads, 'My dear Uzman, return the Orb to me, and 10,000 Gold Pieces will be yours to keep, together with your freedom. And, should my brother meet with an untimely end at your victory ceremony, Blood Island will be yours! Baron Sukumvit.' You put away the note and search the Assassin to find a small phial of clear liquid in her pocket. If you want to drink the liquid, turn to **369**. If you want to leave the chamber by the door at the back, turn to **392**.

210

The helmet slips easily over your head. It's heavy, but feels like it will protect you from heavy blows to the head. But, when you try to take it off, you find it impossible to do so. It has been cursed with evil magic, and it will remain on your head for seven days. Lose 1 LUCK point. You are wearing the Helmet of Hades that will blur your vision in battle. Lose 2 SKILL points. If you have not done so already, you can look at the shield (turn to **325**) or, if you want to leave the room and continue walking up the tunnel, turn to **86**.

211

As soon as you put the ring on your finger, the Golden Dragon door begins to close. If you want to run back out of the chamber before the door closes, turn to **350**. If you want to remain in the chamber, turn to **264**. If you want to walk over to the throne to pick up the Orb, turn to **228**.

212

You check the box for traps, and, satisfied there isn't one, you slowly lift the lid. Inside, you find a silver key lying on top of a green silk cushion. Add 1 LUCK point. You take the key and await your next instruction, but the room remains silent. If you want to open another box, turn to **388**. If you want to open the door, turn to **165**.

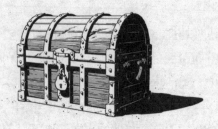

213

The stone floor rises back up with the spectators clapping and cheering wildly. 'I told you I had to be the anchor,' the Priestess says, looking very pleased with herself. 'A little magic can make a big difference.' The officer raises his sword to silence the crowd, telling your team to stand in a line. He turns back to the crowd and says, 'I'm sure you will all agree that this has been a glorious contest so far. To end this part of it, Lord Carnuss will say a few words.' Carnuss rises slowly to his feet and, with a look of satisfaction on his face, says, 'Indeed, this has been a glorious day and I, for one, do not want it to end. So, there will be an additional contest called Life or Death. It will be one-on-one combat that will better reflect the name of my arena. The twelve will become six. Only these six survivors will enter my dungeon!' The spectators go wild on hearing his announcement. Carnuss slowly surveys the twelve remaining competitors. 'Contestants, draw your weapons and prepare to fight to the death. The Dwarf Warrior will fight the Rogue, the Assassin will fight the Berserker, the Monk will fight the Barbarian, the Priestess will fight the Thief, the Warrior-Knight will fight the Mercenary, and the Man-Orc will fight the Adventurer!' he growls in a cold voice, pointing his finger at you. 'Let battle commence!' He sits down to watch the spectacle begin, signalling to the officer to instruct the contestants to stand opposite their opponents. You walk over to the tall MAN-ORC who looks like he is a mean and ferocious fighter. Holding his heavy broadsword in two hands above his head, he charges at you the moment the trumpet sounds. You raise your sword and stand ready to fight him!

MAN-ORC   *SKILL* 8   *STAMINA* 7

If you win, turn to **69**.

The entrance is made of copper in the shape of a demon's head

214

You slide down the long chute, and land with a bump on the ground outside in bright sunlight. There is a huge crowd gathered who cheer loudly when they see you, but their cheers turn to jeers when they find out that you failed in your quest to find the Golden Orb. You are pelted with rotten eggs and tomatoes and have to be rescued by the guards. You are marched to the harbour and put on a boat to take you back to the mainland. Your adventure is over.

215

You set off east and notice that the passageway becomes wider, and the ceiling becomes higher. The passageway soon makes a sharp left turn, and you walk north until you come to a tunnel in the right-hand wall that has an entrance in the shape of the head of a horned demon. It is made of copper that has turned bluish green with verdigris, and its open mouth is big enough to step through. There are burning torches on either side of the entrance and a large brass gong hanging in its wooden frame next to it. If you want to continue walking north, turn to **138**. If you want to enter the new tunnel, turn to **362**. If you want to ring the gong with the striker, turn to **92**.

216

You take a deep breath and open the book. The first chapters are histories of good and evil Wizards, Sorcerers and Necromancers. The other chapters feature lavish illustrations of ingredients that you think are for making potions. Frustratingly, most of the words are in Elvish, which you are unable to read. But there is some mysterious handwriting in large red letters on the last page of the book that you are able to understand. If you want to utter the words 'Skoob Edils Tuo', turn to **66**. If you want to put the book back on the shelf, and you have not done so already, you can either open the book entitled *Dead and Undead* (turn to **248**) or open the book entitled *Dungeon of Despair* (turn to **152**). If you want to leave the library and continue up the corridor, turn to **179**.

217

The Assassin jumps over the pit and says, 'You don't need to answer. I'm true to my word, and I'm going to help you now. Then we are quits. Understand?' You nod in agreement and throw your rope up to her. She wraps it round her waist and tells you to climb up. Once out of the pit, she hands the rope back to you, and you stand facing each other in silence for a few moments. The Assassin holds her hand out and says, 'Shall we join forces for a while?' If you want to shake her hand and join her, turn to **159**. If you want to decline her offer, turn to **282**.

218

You take the skull out of your backpack and walk over to place it in position on top of the Skeleton's spine. It fits perfectly and activates the ORC SKELETON, which starts walking around the room in jerky movements with its skull slowly turning from side to side as though it is looking for something. It stops when it gets to the middle of the room and raises its arms in the air. The ceiling continues to slide down, but grinds to a halt when it touches the Orc Skeleton's outstretched fingers. You hear a creaking sound and fear another trap has been sprung, but it is the noise of the door opening behind you. If you want to leave the room immediately, turn to **249**. If you want to take the silver armband from the Orc Skeleton before leaving, turn to **53**.

219

You see a glass object on the floor, which is partially hidden by the Snakes. But, before you can find out what it is, more Snakes slither over to you and rear up to attack. If you want to stand and fight, turn to **372**. If you want to climb up the ladder to open the door, turn to **110**.

220

You just manage to jump out of the way of the long tongue as it lashes out to snare you. When it recoils into the Bloodbeast's gaping maw, ready to strike again, you seize your chance and slam the door shut in its face. There is a noxious smell of gas coming from the Bloodbeast's lair, and you lock the door for good measure and head north. Turn to **101**.

221

You place the marble cat on the tray and watch the Ghost-Witch stroke the small figure with her spidery hands. 'I'm so happy. Lawrence was gone too long,' she whispers softly. 'You have been very kind to me, unlike one of the other scavengers who I had to cast a spell of Undeath on. You might see him rotting away in the dungeon somewhere. As for you, you may take two of my treasures as a reward for bringing Lawrence back to me.' With a sigh of relief, you examine the items on her tray, which are an Orc skull with curved tusks, a small brass pig, a small silver shoe, a large pebble with a painting of a sword on it, a Gold Piece, a small bottle containing pink sand, a bone die and an empty silk purse. After putting two of the items in your backpack, the Ghost-Witch glides past you down the staircase and along the passageway before disappearing left round the corner. If you want to climb to the top of the staircase, turn to **327**. If you want to go back down the steps and turn right at the junction, turn to **265**.

222

There is a brass plate attached to the door that has a small slot in the middle of it. There is a message etched in the brass plate above the slot, which says 'Insert 1 Gold Piece to open the door'. You try the handle and discover that the door is locked. If you want to put 1 Gold Piece in the slot, turn to **301**. If you want to turn round and head north, turn to **279**.

223

The arrow fired by Thump flies over your head. Having never learned how to use a bow, his arrow misses you by some distance. Alas, he is not so fortunate. Your aim is accurate, and your arrow strikes home. You watch him sink slowly to his knees, holding his stomach where the arrow is protruding from it. He stares at you coldly, his teeth clenched shut in pain. Lose 2 LUCK points. Filled with remorse, you barely notice the noise of the spectators or the groans of the injured contestants. The trumpet blasts out again, and the officer instructs the survivors to line up against the wall opposite him. The injured contestants are led away, and the dead are dragged out of the arena by Carnuss's guards. You watch poor Thump stagger away slowly, head bowed, his contest over. Turn to **83**.

224

You walk downhill for what seems like ages until you eventually arrive at the flooded entrance of a dark cavern with a low ceiling. The water comes from a natural spring and is crystal clear. You drink the cool water and feel immediately refreshed. Add 2 STAMINA points. You can't see a way out of the cavern and walk back up the tunnel to the junction and turn right to head north. Turn to **87**.

225

You sit down in the chair, expecting a boost of energy to surge through your body, when you suddenly sink down as though the seat was made of sponge. The chair metamorphoses into a giant ball of sticky amber jelly that completely envelops you! You have been caught by a GLUGG, a gigantic gelatinous slug that can imitate nearby objects. You find it difficult to breathe or move inside the Glugg, and your skin feels like it is blistering. Lose 2 STAMINA points. You will have to act fast before its gastric fluid starts to dissolve your flesh. If you have a bottle of Weezle Juice, turn to **194**. If you do not have this potion, turn to **16**.

226

The Dragonmaster picks up his dice and says coldly, 'That is unfortunate. The game will now begin. We shall roll our dice. I will roll first.' Roll three dice for the Dragonmaster and compare the total to the total of the dice you roll for yourself. If your dice roll is higher than the total of the Dragonmaster's three dice, turn to **357**. If the number is the same or less than the total of the Dragonmaster's three dice, turn to **55**.

227

When the Hobgoblin sees you draw your sword, he runs off quickly down the tunnel you came from, laughing hysterically. You give chase and see him unlock and open one of the iron doors and slam it shut behind him. When you reach the door, you find it is firmly locked. Lose 1 LUCK point. You have no choice but to walk back through the cavern to the archways. Turn to **393**.

228

You pick up the Orb and discover that it's not made of solid gold. It's hollow and not as heavy as it looks. You shake it and hear something metallic rattle inside. You hold it up and admire the detail of the two dragons curved round it. Smoke suddenly shoots out from the nostrils of the dragons and swirls round your head. You step away from the throne, but the smoke continues to

The room is filled with burning candles

circle about your head, making it difficult to breathe. You drop the Orb and hear it smash on the floor. You run round the chamber, coughing uncontrollably, but are unable to rid yourself of the circle of smoke. You begin to choke as you inhale more smoke and drop to your knees. You slump forward, and, as you lose consciousness, you see that the Orb is nothing more than a gold-painted ceramic ball. There is a small bronze figure of Lord Carnuss lying among the pieces of broken pottery, pointing at you. It is the last thing you see before you lose consciousness forever. Your adventure is over.

229

The door opens into a warmly lit room that is filled with burning candles on the floor, and on furniture, in bottles, candlesticks, saucers, plates, curios and skulls, all dripping melting wax everywhere. You pick up a bone die off the floor, but nothing else catches your eye except for a helmet on a small shelf on the left side of the back wall and an ornate round shield made of polished steel hanging on the right side of the wall. If you want to look at the helmet, turn to **139**. If you want to look at the shield, turn to **325**. If you want to close the door and keep walking, turn to **86**.

230

The passageway continues straight on, and you soon arrive at a narrow staircase where you go down a long flight of stone steps to another passageway. Continuing north, the passageway opens out into a cavern that has a water well in the centre of it. Beyond the well, you see another passageway in the far wall. There is a small bell hanging on the wall of the well next to a sign that says:

> *Drop a Gold Piece and ring the bell*
> *For words of wisdom from the well*

If you want to ring the bell and have a Gold Piece to drop into the well, turn to **269**. If you would rather walk over to the new passageway, turn to **376**.

231

The Bronze Warrior strides slowly towards you with its sword raised ready to strike.

BRONZE WARRIOR   SKILL 9   STAMINA 10

If you win an Attack Round, your sword will only reduce the Warrior's STAMINA by 1 point. If you possess a Craggen Knife, it will reduce the Warrior's STAMINA by 2 points when you win an Attack Round. If you win, turn to **4**. You may Escape, but you must lose 2 STAMINA points as the Warrior will wound you as you flee. Turn to **331**.

232

The tunnel soon turns sharply right, and, as you walk along in the dim light, the ceiling becomes lower and lower until you reach a point where you have to keep your head down to avoid hitting it. You become aware of a putrid smell like rotten eggs and begin to feel light-headed and dizzy. You find it difficult to walk in a straight line and start bumping into the walls. Suddenly you pass out, landing on your face on the tunnel floor. You have inhaled toxic gas. Lose 3 STAMINA points. If you are still alive, you wake up to find that you still have all your possessions apart from one of your Provisions, which was eaten by a Rat. You stagger on and at last reach a T-junction. The cross tunnel is much bigger than the one you are in. Looking right, you see that the tunnel heads south for some distance. Looking left, the tunnel goes on for twenty metres to where there is a stairway going down. You hear sharp footsteps and see an armoured SKELETON appear on the steps. When it nears the top, you see that it is dragging a huge glowing sword behind it and is struggling with the weight of it. The sword looks special, and you decide to fight the Skeleton to get it. You rush forward to attack the Skeleton, which looks barely able to lift the sword over its head.

SKELETON	*SKILL* 5	*STAMINA* 6

If you win, turn to **78**.

233

You run to the Dwarf's aid and see there is a dagger sticking out of his back and blood seeping from his leather armour. He sees you and coughs. 'What took you so long to get here,' he says slowly, spitting blood, his face contorted with pain. 'I'm done for, my friend. I'm not sure who did it. It might have been the ice-cold Assassin or that slime rat, Uzman Koh. I never trusted either of them... Curses to them... It's too late for me, but there are some things in my pockets that you'll want... Take them... And under my helmet... there's a...' His eyes suddenly widen as he draws in his last breath and slowly exhales. His head slumps forward and you realize there is nothing you can do for poor Thump. You find 2 Gold Pieces in one pocket and two charms in the other pocket, one a four-leaf clover and the other a small horseshoe. If you want to take off his helmet, turn to **322**. If you want to leave him where he is and carry on walking down the corridor, turn to **6**.

234

You stand opposite the Barbarian, who stares at you coldly. The gates open and an ox-drawn cart piled high with large iron balls rolls slowly into the arena. The officer instructs everybody to take an iron ball from the cart and hold it above their head opposite their partner. The ball is heavy, and you have difficulty lifting it above your head. The Barbarian lifts his ball without much effort. The crowd cheers as iron balls thud into the ground all around the arena with the eliminated contestants led away by the guards. The muscles in your arms start to burn and tremble under the weight of the ball, and you wonder how much longer you can last. Lose 2 STAMINA points. You glance at the Barbarian, whose grimacing face is now dripping with sweat. Turn to **149**.

235

Remembering the Hobgoblin's advice, you tell the Juggler that you will sit down for a rest, but need a drink of water first. You reach into your backpack and pretend to pull out your water bottle, but instead grab the handbell. You ring it furiously, which makes him cry out and cover his ears. He barges past you and runs screaming down the tunnel. You watch him disappear and decide what to do. If you want to sit down on the bench, turn to **293**. If you want to head west, turn to **123**. If you want to head east, turn to **334**.

236

You soon arrive at another T-junction where the cross tunnel has been built with large stone walls and a stone floor that is covered with a thin layer of sand. Looking left, you see the tunnel goes straight on before disappearing into the gloom. Looking right, you see the tunnel goes straight on for about twenty metres before turning left. The footprints you saw earlier head east at this point. If you want to turn right and head east, turn to **77**. If you want to turn left and head west, turn to **333**.

237

Heading north, you soon arrive at the entrance to a narrow tunnel in the right-hand wall, which you notice has a rough stone floor sloping downwards. If you want to walk east down the new tunnel, turn to **224**. If you want to carry on walking north, turn to **87**.

238

Holding your sword at the ready, you walk slowly up the narrow spiral staircase that leads to the beginning of a narrow corridor heading south. There are burning torches set along the stone walls at regular intervals, and ahead you can see a wooden door in the right-hand wall. If you want to open the door, turn to **79**. If you would rather walk on past the door, turn to **331**.

239

If you have placed four keys on the table, turn to **381**. If you have placed less than four keys on the table, turn to **175**.

240

The Monk frowns and says, 'I've just come from up there. There's nothing to see apart from rubble. It's a dead end.' If you want to change your mind and join the Monk, turn to **178**. If you still want to head east, turn to **356**.

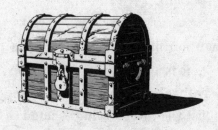

241

You just manage to grab hold of the rope handrail, but can't stop yourself from falling through the gap in the bridge and are left dangling by one arm over the abyss. Roll one die. If you roll a 1, turn to **120**. If you roll 2–6, turn to **14**.

242

The passageway is well lit and has smooth walls and a mosaic floor with the small pieces of tile laid down in a pattern of flying dragons. You walk along it slowly, ever mindful of hidden traps. The passageway ends at a bronze door that opens into a small, tomb-like room with a pyramid-shaped ceiling. There is another bronze door in the wall opposite on which there is a large knocker cast in the shape of a dragon. In the centre of the room is a square stone plinth with a dragon's head carved on each face. The plinth is the base for a stone hand that is holding a Golden Orb in its palm. You can hardly believe your eyes and walk round the plinth, inspecting it carefully for traps. You don't find any and decide to lift the Orb out of the stone hand. Turn to **387**.

243

You follow the tunnel east and arrive at a low, narrow archway. There is a tall, narrow wooden box on one side of the archway that has an old sword sticking out of the top of it with just the hilt showing. There is a sign attached to the wall on the other side of the archway that says, 'No swords allowed beyond this point. Place all swords in the box provided. Failure to do so will result in death.' If you want to put your sword in the wooden box, turn to **44**. If you want to walk through the archway, holding your sword, turn to **125**. If you would rather turn round and go back to the junction to head west, turn to **80**.

244

244

The Barbarian's feet slide out from under him, but he manages to regain his footing without letting go of the rope. You are pulled forward slightly with the Man-Orc cursing loudly behind you. Without warning, the Priestess lets go of the rope with one hand and points to the sky. A green flash sparks from her ring finger, and the rope immediately feels easier to pull, as though an invisible hand is helping you pull it. You start to inch your way backwards, and your wailing and grunting opponents cannot stop themselves from being pulled towards you. The officer suddenly raises his sword to signal you have dragged them forward by a metre. The stone floor gives way beneath them, and you watch them fall into the void, screaming in terror. Turn to **213**.

There are skulls hanging on long spikes nailed to the wall

245

A search of the Troll Guard's pockets produces nothing more than a dried pig's ear and a snot-filled rag it was using as a handkerchief. You look inside the Troll's rancid-smelling room and see creature skulls hanging on long spikes nailed to the back wall. There is a battered iron chest on the floor, a crude wooden bed in one corner, a bucket and ladle, and a plate of bread and mouldy cheese next to a jug of water on a table. At the back of the room, you see a heavy wooden door that is bolted shut with iron bars across it, secured with large padlocks. There is an eye carved on the door and an iron key hanging on a nail below it. Will you:

Open the iron chest?	Turn to **385**
Try to open the door at the back of the room?	Turn to **67**
Eat the bread and cheese?	Turn to **168**
Close the door and walk on?	Turn to **230**
Close the door, run back down the staircase and turn right at the junction?	Turn to **265**

246

You start hacking at the door frantically with your hand axe with the ceiling now no more than two metres above the floor. *Test Your Luck*. If you are Lucky, turn to **363**. If you are Unlucky, turn to **49**.

247

You wish the Gnome good luck and head north. The passageway goes on as far as you can see, and you walk on for some distance until your foot comes into contact with what sounds like a metal plate. A chill runs down your spine, and you look up to see a large section of the ceiling dropping down. There is no time to jump out of the way, and you are crushed beneath the stone slab. Your adventure is over.

248

The pages in the book are yellow and brittle, and some fall apart when you touch them. The book is full of descriptions and illustrations of undead creatures and tortured souls. On the centre pages, there is a pen-and-ink illustration of a longhaired man in tattered clothing who is chained to a dungeon wall with his head bowed. There are some words below the illustration, in a language you do not understand, which read 'Nush-Na-Ma-Gar'. If you want to say the words out loud, turn to **307**. If you want to close the book and leave the library to continue up the corridor, turn to **179**.

249

You walk on until you reach a T-junction where the passageway joins a much larger tunnel that is lit by burning torches. Looking left, the tunnel heads west as far as you can see. Looking right, you see somebody in the distance walking slowly towards you. If you want to head west, turn to **80**. If you want to see who is coming down the tunnel, turn to **15**.

250

As you are pulled towards the Bloodbeast, you draw your knife with your free hand and hack at the bulbous tongue. It slides off your arm and draws back inside its gaping maw. You seize your chance and slam the door shut in its face. There is a noxious smell of gas coming from the Bloodbeast's lair, and you lock the door for good measure and head north. Turn to **101**.

251

The door isn't locked and opens into a dimly lit tunnel running left and right, which has rough stone walls, hewn out of the rock by Carnuss's slaves. The air is cool and dank, and there is an eerie silence save for the occasional clang of a bell coming from a long way off. You peer into the gloom and decide which way to go. If you want to head west, turn to **7**. If you want to head east in the direction of the sound of the bell, turn to **328**.

252

Seeing nobody beyond the archway, you step through it to retrieve your sword. The old sword is still in the box, but your own sword has gone. Lose 1 LUCK point. You have no choice but to take the old sword, which has a blunt blade and a loose hilt. If you use this sword in combat, deduct 1 point from your Attack Strength. You walk off, muttering to yourself, passing the Warrior-Knight's body, before reaching the junction where you continue on, heading west. Turn to **80**.

253

The gauntlets glide past you and begin scratching manically at the door with their steel-tipped fingers. The door suddenly opens on its own, and the gauntlets immediately turn and go back down the tunnel. You seize your chance and slip through the open door. Turn to **173**.

254

The Woodcutter looks disappointed and says, 'I thought you would know the answer. Anyway, I must bid you farewell as I still have a lot of logs to chop. I wish you well on your quest.' He gestures towards the door for you to leave and raises his axe to chop another log. If you want to attack the Woodcutter, turn to **37**. If you would rather leave the room and carry on walking up the corridor, turn to **386**.

255

There is nothing in the room that is of use to you other than the shield. If you don't already have a shield, you sling it over your shoulder and leave the room to head north along the passageway. Turn to **154**.

256

You swing on the rope towards the tunnel, but spin round and hit your head hard on the wall. If you are not wearing a helmet, lose 2 STAMINA points. The Troglodyte fires its slingshot again and does not miss at this range. Lose 2 STAMINA points. Injured and exhausted, you somehow drag yourself up the rope to escape. You climb out of the well and, with nothing else to see in the cavern, you hurry over to the new passageway in case the Troglodyte returns with reinforcements. Turn to **376**.

257

You watch Thump run across the white line to join his team. The contestants on your side look strong and confident too, with a Berserker, two Pirates and a giant of a Warrior among them. With the teams established, a party of gangly slaves enters the arena, carrying shovels. They begin digging out the sand on both sides of the white line to reveal two long sections of solid stone floor. When they are finished, more slaves enter the arena, carrying a long length of thick rope. They lay it lengthways across both sections of stone floor with half of it on one side of the chalk line and half of it on the other side. 'A Line in the Sand is a Tug-of-War contest. It will be the final contest in the arena,' the officer announces triumphantly to rapturous applause from the crowd. 'Take your positions on the rope.' The Berserker takes up the lead position, and the huge Warrior walks to the back of the line to be the anchor. You take a middle position with the Pirates. Gripping the rope tightly, everybody leans back to take up the strain. The officer raises his sword and shouts, 'When I say heave, pull on the rope as hard as you can! The first team to drag the other team forward by a metre will be judged the winner. Get ready! One, two, three – heave!' Sweating profusely in the heat, you lean as far back as you can, pulling on the rope with all your might. The minutes pass with neither team able to pull the other forward. Suddenly you see the Priestess on Thump's team let go of the rope and point to the sky. A green flash sparks from her ring finger. The rope immediately feels harder to pull, as though an invisible hand is helping the other side. You are dragged forward, and there is nothing you can do to stop it. The officer raises his sword to signal you have been dragged forward by a metre. The stone floor beneath gives way, and you and your team falls into the void, screaming in terror. Your adventure is over.

258

You toss the coin up and watch it spin in the air. *Test Your Luck*. If you are Lucky, turn to **46**. If you are Unlucky, turn to **287**.

259

You are knocked down and run over by the Spikle, but the breastplate takes the brunt of the impact. The Imp loses control and crashes his Spikle into the stone wall. Lose 2 STAMINA points and gain 1 LUCK point. You get to your feet, bruised and breathing hard. You see the Imp stand up and grab his spiked club. If you want to talk to the Imp, turn to **10**. If you want to fight him, turn to **164**.

260

There is a coil of rope hanging on a nail on the back of the door. You throw one end of the rope down to the Assassin who catches it with her outstretched hands. You pull her out of the pit and watch her wipe the Spider blood off the tip of her spear. She stands there silently for a few moments before saying coldly, 'I am an Assassin, and we are competitors. But I owe you now, and if we meet again I will give you my help should you need it. But only once. What you find in this room is yours in payment for saving my life.' With that, she turns and leaves the room, slamming the door behind her. You coil up the rope and sling it over your shoulder before looking at the chalice.

A gargantuan beast appears from out of the gloom

Inside, you find a small solid silver ball that is etched with a dragon motif and a small tin labelled Worm Paste. You put the items in your backpack and leave the room to carry on up the tunnel. Turn to **124**.

261

The footsteps become quicker and louder, and suddenly a gargantuan beast appears from out of the gloom and stops in front of you, blocking the tunnel. It has a large reptilian head with small eyes fixed on you, and a huge jaw lined with long, spiked teeth. It is standing upright on its powerful back legs, ready to strike. Its long tail swishes slowly from side to side, banging against the walls of the narrow tunnel, which causes dust to fall from the ceiling. It is a RAPTOREX. The creature lets out a deafening roar, and it looks intent on devouring you. There is no escaping the giant predator, and you have no choice but to fight it. If you are fighting with a Doom Sword, add 2 points to your Attack Strength during each Attack Round for this battle only.

RAPTOREX   SKILL 11   STAMINA 10

If you win, turn to **52**.

262

You climb out of the pit and brush all the Cockroaches off your body without realizing that hundreds have crawled inside your backpack. Lose two Provisions if you have any remaining. You clear the stinking insects out of your backpack and follow the tunnel west for another thirty minutes before it turns right and heads north. Turn to **112**.

263

When you take the book off the shelf, it begins to give off a shimmering green glow. If you still want to open the book, turn to **216**. If you want to put the book back on the shelf and you have not done so already, you can either open the book entitled *Dead and Undead* (turn to **248**) or open the book entitled *Dungeon of Despair* (turn to **152**). If you want to leave the library and continue up the corridor, turn to **179**.

264

You watch the heavy door slam shut. If you want to walk over to the door to find out if it is locked, turn to **337**. If you want to walk over to the throne to pick up the Orb, turn to **228**.

265

You soon reach the doorway in the left-hand wall of the tunnel. The door isn't locked, and it opens into a circular room that has red walls lined with burning torches. There are three small, round tables in the room, each with a wooden box on top. The tables all have brass feet that resemble dragon claws. There is a circular iron plate on the floor in the middle of the room with the words 'Stand Here' written on it in white letters. If you want to stand on the iron plate, turn to **347**. If you would rather close the door and continue walking up the tunnel, turn to **198**.

266

Roll two dice. If the total is equal to or less than your SKILL score, turn to **26**. If the number is greater than your SKILL score, turn to **131**.

267

Much to your relief, you see the Thief's legs buckle underneath him. He drops his iron ball and curses loudly as it thumps into the ground. Not a moment too soon, you drop your ball and shout out in triumph as the Thief is led away. You are exhausted, and the muscles in your arms are burning. Lose 1 STAMINA point. You are relieved to have won the contest and look around to see how Thump has fared. Turn to **310**.

268

You drink the contents of the bottle, but don't feel any effects from it. If you have not done so already, you can put the bone ring on your finger (turn to **330**). If you do not want to wear the ring, you can continue east (turn to **243**) or turn round and go back to the junction to head west (turn to **80**).

269

The bell makes a sharp tinkling sound that echoes round the cavern. You toss the Gold Piece in the well and suddenly hear a sniggering voice say, 'My wise words are: don't believe anything you read in this dungeon!' You look down the well and see a small Goblin-like creature in a loincloth looking up at you from the mouth of a tunnel halfway down the wall. He has a big nose and very long ears. He's a TROGLODYTE. He waves your Gold Piece at you and disappears, laughing loudly. There is a rope on a winch hanging down the well with a bucket tied to it. If you want to slide down the rope to the tunnel entrance, turn to **153**. If you would rather walk over to the new passageway, turn to **376**.

270

You insert the key in the lock and hear it turn. The Dragonmaster nods his head in acknowledgement. 'Congratulations. Just one more lock to open. The problem is, I can't let you open the door and walk out of here just like that,' he says coldly, snatching the remaining key off the table. 'Should you escape from this dungeon with the Golden Orb, you will become hideously rich, whereas I must survive on whatever pittance Lord Carnuss deigns to give me. So, I'm looking to you for a small gratuity for allowing you to progress. You have two choices. One, you give me all your Gold Pieces, and I will give you your key back. Or two, you die a hero.' If you want to give the Dragonmaster all your treasure and gold, turn to **294**. If you want to attack the Dragonmaster, turn to **38**.

271

You walk back down the tunnel past the junction on your left, and it doesn't take long for you to catch up with the Monk, who tells you he is pleased that you changed your mind and joined forces with him. Turn to **178**.

272

The door opens into a large room that appears to be an old library. There are floor-to-ceiling wooden bookcases lining the walls and bookshelves set in rows on the floor, all crammed with dusty leather-bound books. There is a musty smell in the cool air. Cobwebs hang from the shelves, and the floor is littered with paper and debris. If you want to look at some of the books, turn to **31**. If you would rather close the door and carry on up the corridor, turn to **179**.

273

The Dwarf breathes a sigh of relief and introduces himself as Diggle from Mirewater. He tells you he has been wandering around the dungeon for days. He was dropped into the dungeon against his will by Carnuss's henchmen as a test to see if the dungeon was secure enough. 'I can tell you it is,' he says, grimacing. 'I keep being attacked by vile creatures and there are Troll Guards everywhere. Miraculously, I am still alive, but not for much longer, I fear. I'm tired, I'm hungry and I want to go home. Do you have any food you could give to me? I've got nothing to pay you with, but I have something that might be useful to you.' If you want to give Diggle one of your Provisions, turn to **64**. If you do not want to give him any food, or don't have any to give, turn to **339**.

274

Tripping over the wire triggers small, needle-sharp iron spikes to shoot up from holes in the stone floor. You stumble forward in the darkness, but somehow avoid stepping on a spike. You walk on slowly, watching out carefully for more traps. Turn to **62**.

275

You clutch at thin air and can't stop yourself from falling through the gap in the bridge. You fall headlong into the ravine and land on a bed of rocks thirty metres below. Your adventure is over.

The horned creature has spikes running down its back and tail

276

When you place the Dragon Balls on the table, the Dragonmaster says in a sombre voice, 'Finding three Dragon Balls is a good effort, but you still have a very difficult task ahead of you. Follow me.' He walks over to the first iron door in the right-hand wall and unlocks it. He opens the door and beckons you to walk through, saying, 'If you survive, knock on the door. I'll be waiting for you.' You draw your sword and walk into a dank, dark cave. You hear the door slam shut behind you and see a tall green-skinned creature with a reptilian head walking towards you. It has a ridge of spikes along its back and its long tail, and two horns on its head. It is wearing body armour and is carrying a long spear. It is a LIZARD MAN, and you must fight it.

| LIZARD MAN | SKILL 8 | STAMINA 9 |

If you win, turn to **32**.

277

The key turns in the lock, but, as you reach for the handle, the door bursts open! Two creatures with long, whiskered snouts poking out of their hooded robes run out, squeaking loudly in high-pitched voices. They are RATMEN armed with short swords, and you ready yourself to fight them one at a time.

First RATMAN	SKILL 5	STAMINA 5
Second RATMAN	SKILL 5	STAMINA 4

If you win, turn to **5**.

278

Thump counts the raised hands and says, 'That's five in favour of the Priestess and seven in favour of the Man-Orc. The Man-Orc will be our anchor.' Everybody takes up their position on the rope with the Barbarian at the front, with you and Thump in second and third position and the Man-Orc at the back. You watch the opposing team take their positions on the rope with a Berserker at the front and a giant of a Warrior at the back as their anchor. Gripping the rope tightly, you lean back to take up the strain, sweating profusely in the heat. The officer raises his sword and shouts, 'When I say heave, pull on the rope as hard as you can! The first team to drag the other team forward by a metre will be judged the winner. Get ready! One, two, three – heave!' Sweating profusely in the heat, but encouraged by the grimacing faces of your opponents, you lean as far back as you can, pulling on the rope with all your might. *Test Your Luck*. If you are Lucky, turn to **244**. If you are Unlucky, turn to **35**.

279

You soon arrive at a heavy oak door set in a reinforced doorway in the right-hand wall. There is a key in the door and a brass plate attached to the front panel with a message etched on it that reads 'Do not open'. If you want to open the door, turn to **162**. If you want to carry on walking along the tunnel, turn to **101**.

280

One of the Vampire Bats was carrying PARASITES. *Test Your Luck*. If you are Lucky, turn to **73**. If you are Unlucky, turn to **314**.

281

The Goblin's aim is true, and his dagger strikes your shoulder. Lose 2 STAMINA points. You pull the dagger out and, before he has time to throw another dagger at you, you run forward and launch a double-footed dropkick at the Goblin that sends him and his fellow Guard tumbling down the stairwell, screaming loudly. You run down after them and find them lying in a heap, unconscious on the cavern floor. You rummage through their belongings and find two throwing daggers, a brass button, a small bottle of Mullweed Oil, a rabbit's-foot charm and a piece of stale bread. You eat the bread (gain 1 STAMINA point) and take what items you need before walking through the archway into the tunnel to head east. Turn to **207**.

282

You tell the Assassin that you want to continue the quest on your own. 'So be it,' she says coldly. 'We are now enemies, but let's not spill our blood fighting each other here.' You agree to split up at the next junction and walk on together until you come to a new passageway in the right-hand wall. 'I choose which way to go since I just saved you,' she says forcefully. 'I'm going to head north. Good luck.' You watch her disappear up the new tunnel before continuing westwards. Turn to **366**.

283

You conquer you fear and step forward to fight the vile creature as it tries to rip you apart with its four clawed hands in a frenzied attack. If you are fighting with a Vorpal Sword, add 2 points to your Attack Strength during each Attack Round for this battle only.

HOWLING DEMON   *SKILL* 12   *STAMINA* 10

Deduct 3 STAMINA points instead of 2 points each time the Demon wins an Attack Round. If you win, turn to **367**.

284

He looks at you intently with piercing eyes and says, 'If you want to stay alive, don't choose five.' Before you have time to ask him to explain, he disappears into the crowd. You tell Thump what the man said, but he dismisses it as nonsense, saying, 'What's he talking about? Number five? Number five what? Forget it.' Thump turns and walks on, waving at everybody and soaking up the adulation from his growing number of fans. You hear a shrill whistle and turn to see a tall man in a hooded cloak looking at you. He pulls a long knife out from under his cloak and waves it in the air. If you want to speak to the man, turn to **91**. If you want to ignore him and catch up with Thump, turn to **12**.

285

The Dwarf puts his swords down and backs away. 'Stop! Stop! You win!' he yells. 'Maybe I was a bit hasty in attacking you, but you can't blame me. You said you were my foe!' You suddenly feel sorry for the Dwarf and tell him to be on his away. He trudges off, nursing his wounds and mumbling to himself. You continue walking along the tunnel, and it's not long before you come to a dead end where a rockfall has blocked the passageway. There is nothing there except for the smouldering remains of a campfire, and all you can do is turn round and exit the tunnel. You are soon back at the copper mouth and turn right to head north up the passageway. Turn to **138**.

286

You just manage to jump to the side and avoid being run down by the Imp who doesn't stop and carries on riding his Spikle down the corridor. 'I'll get you next time, wormbrain!' he shouts and starts laughing hysterically. The laughter soon dies away, and you set off again, now heading north. Turn to **104**.

287

You watch the coin land on the floor. It's a tail. When you reach down to pick it up, you hear a mystery voice behind you utter the chilling words, 'What gold was yours is now mine.' You search your pockets and backpack and discover that all your Gold Pieces have vanished! There is nothing you can do but continue up the passageway, cursing your luck. Turn to **348**.

288

While holding the door handle, a small Spider hidden in a crevice above the door suddenly drops down on its silk thread and sinks its fangs into the back of your hand. Its bite is poisonous! Lose 2 STAMINA points. You brush the Spider off your hand and stamp on it. Unable to open the iron door, you have no choice but to turn round and walk back in the direction of the sound of the bell. Turn to **328**.

289

You try to jump out of the way of the long tongue as it lashes out, but it wraps itself round one of your arms, squeezing it tightly. Lose 1 STAMINA point. If you possess a Craggen Knife, turn to **250**. If you do not own this knife, turn to **157**.

290

The burning pain becomes intolerable, and you pass out due to lack of oxygen. You are being slowly digested by the Glugg and never regain consciousness. Your adventure is over.

291

After all the contestants have selected their partners, the officer announces with gusto, 'Bull's Eye is an archery contest! I hope you have chosen wisely because the targets for this contest are the contestants!' He sniggers, hardly able to contain himself. The spectators gasp in shock. You look at Thump and shake your head. He stares back at you with a deep frown on his face. 'Form yourselves into two lines of fifty-five contestants, making sure you stand opposite your partner, thirty paces apart. You will be given a bow, and you must fire the arrow at your partner when you hear the trumpet sound. Anybody who is hit by an arrow will be eliminated, some fatally so.' You have no choice but to take your place in the line to face Thump.

The haggard-looking old woman is carrying a skull on a tray

Guards enter the arena to hand out the bows and arrows to the contestants. You see Thump's arrow aimed at you, and, in two minds as to what to do, you take aim and await the sound of the trumpet. The crowd roars as the trumpet blasts out a high-pitched note. If you want to fire your arrow at Thump, turn to **335**. If you want to aim over his head, turn to **202**.

292

A ghostly apparition suddenly appears at the top of the stairs. Standing motionless in the gloom is a haggard-looking old woman with a disturbing expression on her face. She has long, straggly white hair and is wearing long, baggy robes tied at the waist. She appears to be carrying a skull on a tray. When you take a step up, she takes a step down. When you stop, she stops. If you want to carry on climbing up the staircase, turn to **34**. If you want to go back down and turn right at the junction, turn to **265**.

293

You sit down on the bench and fall asleep immediately. You wake up ten minutes later feeling alert and energized. Add 2 STAMINA points. You stand up and decide which way to go. If you want to head west, turn 123. If you want to head east, turn 334.

294

The Dragonmaster examines the items on the table and hands the key to you, saying, 'I was hoping for more, but this will have to do.' Deduct the items you give to the Dragonmaster from your *Adventure Sheet*. 'You may now leave my chamber. Did I tell you that there are three Demons on the other side of the door? No, I don't think I did. Sorry, it must have slipped my mind. Anyway, good luck with them!' If you want to open the fourth lock, turn to the paragraph with the same number as the key. If you do not know the number on the key, turn to **336**. If you want to attack the Dragonmaster to retrieve your treasure items, turn to **38**.

295

When the man finishes chopping the log in half, he puts down his axe and looks at you with a bored expression on his face. 'Not another one,' he sighs. 'I suppose you're looking for the Orb too. Well, it's not here, and I have no idea where it is so don't bother asking. The only information I can give you is about the dungeon itself. But that comes at a cost.' He wipes his forehead and leans on his axe. 'I've been chopping wood all day, and I'm tired and hungry. Are you willing to pay for my information with food?' If you want to give the Woodcutter one of your Provisions, turn to **114**. If you would rather leave the room and carry on walking up the corridor, turn to **386**.

296

Flames bellow from the Lava Demon's mouth as it throws a huge chunk of molten lava at you, forcing you to dive out of the way. Roll two dice. If the total is equal to or less than your SKILL score, turn to **384**. If the number is greater than your SKILL score, turn to **74**.

297

The Ghost-Witch looks suddenly annoyed. 'You'd better go back and look for him then!' she hisses. If you want to ignore the Ghost-Witch's command and walk past her, turn to **391**. If you want to go back down the stairs and turn right at the junction, turn to **265**.

298

She curses loudly and asks you to pull the arrow out of her shoulder. She grits her teeth as you tug on the arrow, but does not utter a sound. You bandage her wound and ask her what she saw. 'There's a lavish chamber on the other side of the doors with big columns and a marble floor with a compass-rose inlay. I didn't see anybody in there, but that arrow wasn't fired by a ghost. We need to charge into the room, split up and attack whoever it is from both sides. Open the door – we're going in.' Turn to **394**.

299

The Thief looks pleased with his final choice of slab and stands with his arms crossed, smiling and nodding to the cheering crowd. The cheers suddenly turn to gasps when Lord Carnuss pulls down on the iron lever and the slabs fall away. You drop through a hole and find yourself sliding down a steep stone chute, landing awkwardly on the floor of a pit. You have sprained your ankle badly and can hardly put any weight on it. Lose 1 SKILL point. The pale light from amber crystals fixed to the wall is enough for you to see a small metal box on a ledge on one side of the pit and an iron door on the opposite side. If you want to open the box, turn to **122**. If you want to open the door, turn to **251**.

300

You notice that the Cyclops has a manacle on its ankle with a long chain attached to it and the other end attached to an iron ring fixed to the floor of its chamber. You slip into its cramped chamber, which reeks of stale sweat. There is a straw mattress in one corner and a wooden bucket in the other. You hear its chain rattle on the floor and look round to see the giant Cyclops standing in the doorway, chewing on a very large bone. It belches loudly and says, 'My house,' before stepping forward to club you with the huge thigh bone.

CYCLOPS   *SKILL* 10   *STAMINA* 10

If you win, turn to **151**.

301

You hear the coin drop on to a metal plate on the other side of the door. You try the handle again, but it doesn't turn. The door remains firmly locked. You wait for a while and hear footsteps approaching and what sounds like somebody picking up the coin from the plate. You bang on the door, but all that happens is that you hear footsteps again, with whoever it is on the other side of the door walking slowly away. Lose 1 LUCK point. Despite your best efforts, you fail to open the door, and have no choice but to turn round and head north. Turn to **279**.

302

The water is pure and refreshing. Add 2 STAMINA points. While drinking, you notice there is a bronze key at the bottom of the bowl. You take the key, slip it into your pocket and walk on. Turn to **365**.

303

You try to jump out of the way, but the Imp changes direction and ploughs straight into you at high speed. If you are wearing a breastplate, turn to **259**. If you are not wearing a breastplate, turn to **197**.

304

You plunge your sword into the liquid and immediately hear bubbling as toxic vapour rises from the urn. You pull your sword out quickly and curse when you see that the blade has been partly dissolved by the corrosive acid in the urn! Deduct 1 point from your Attack Strength if you use this sword in combat, and lose 1 LUCK point. Mad at yourself for damaging your sword, you stride off down the tunnel. Further along, you stop to look at a large hole in the ceiling when you suddenly hear loud stomping footsteps coming down the tunnel. You draw your sword and stand ready to face the oncoming creature. Turn to **261**.

305

You reach into the hole and catch hold of something cold and metallic. It's a copper key that you slip into your pocket. You try the door handle and are relieved to discover that it turns in your hand. The door opens and you walk down a long, dimly lit tunnel roughly carved out of the rock. The air is cool and dank, and it is eerily quiet. The tunnel ends at an iron door that you unlock with the key. You enter another dimly lit tunnel, passing several more iron doors that don't unlock with the key. You hear the occasional clang of a bell coming down the tunnel from a long way off and have no option but to head in that direction. Turn to **328**.

306

As soon as you touch the scroll, it bursts into flame, and is soon nothing more than black ash held in the clenched fist. You check the walls for hidden doors and secret passages, but find nothing. You decide that your only choice is to walk back to the previous junction and head west. As you turn the corner, you don't notice a small panel in the ceiling drop down. Nor do you see the blowpipe sticking out of it that is aimed at you. *Test Your Luck*. If you are Lucky, turn to **136**. If you are Unlucky, turn to **315**.

307

As soon as you have uttered the words, the illustration starts to move on the page! The man's head lifts, and you see he has a broken jaw and his mouth is hanging open. His sickly-white eyes are bulging and red-rimmed, and his skull has a deep wound in it like it has been struck with an axe. He starts to wrestle with the chains that hold him. If you want to keep the book open, turn to **96**. If you want to close the book and leave the library immediately to continue up the corridor, turn to **179**.

308

You grab the rope and tug on it a few times to see if it will bear your weight. It feels safe enough and, holding the rope with both hands, you take a few steps backwards and run forward to swing over the pit. You land safely on the other

The tall hooded figure is wearing a white face mask

side and walk on, following the tunnel west for another thirty minutes before it turns right and heads north. Turn to **112**.

309

The door opens into a large chamber with a high ceiling where you see a tall figure in hooded robes standing in front of a long wooden table with a heavy oak door behind them. There are two iron doors in the left-hand wall and two in the right-hand wall. On seeing you enter, the hooded figure places both hands on the table and you notice a large gemstone ring on the right forefinger of their gloved hand. You are unable to make out their face as it is hidden by a white face mask. 'You are the first to arrive here. Interesting. I thought it would have been the Warrior-Knight. No matter,' the masked figure says in a deep voice. 'I am the Dragonmaster, the senior servant of Lord Carnuss. I'll say this once. Do not attack me. It would be foolish. To progress, you must pass three tests. The first test is a game. If you win, you will take the second test. If you lose, well, let's just say it's better not to lose. I trust you are prepared for the challenges that await you. Do you have any bone dice? If you do, place them on the table.' If you have one or more bone dice, turn to **324**. If you want to reply that you do not have any bone dice, turn to **18**. If you want to attack the Dragonmaster, turn to **38**.

310

You see Thump nearby, sitting, arms folded, on his iron ball with a beaming smile on his face. 'That wasn't too hard, was it?' he says as you approach him. Before you can answer, the trumpet sounds again, and the officer instructs the remaining twenty-four contestants to gather at one end of the arena. Gates open at the other end, and a guard walks to the middle, carrying a large silver jug. He begins to pour chalk dust on to the sand, marking out a white line across the arena. The officer raises his sword to silence the murmuring crowd. 'The next contest is a team game called A Line in the Sand!' he bellows. 'You must now make another choice. I want twelve of you to be on one side of the chalk line and twelve of you on the other side. Either stay where you are or step over the line. Do it now.' A Pirate, a Man-Orc and a Barbarian run across the line, cheering loudly. They are immediately followed by a Thief and a Priestess. Thump turns to you and says, 'I like their spirit. I'm going to join them. Are you coming?' If you want to follow Thump across the line, turn to **398**. If you want to stay where you are, turn to **257**.

311

Much to your surprise, the door isn't locked. You leave the room and head west along the tunnel. Turn to **198**.

312

You continue to walk uphill until you reach a point where it is almost too steep to carry on. Up ahead, you see what looks like a giant dragon skull made of stone blocking the tunnel. It is held firmly in position by thick chains, making it impossible to squeeze past. You have no option but to walk back to the last junction. You walk quickly downhill and turn left into the new passageway. Turn to **237**.

313

You breathe in deeply as you slide the bracelet over your hand. Nothing happens at first, but suddenly the bracelet shrinks tightly round your wrist, and you are unable to take it off. The Goblin stole it from an old alchemist by the name of Gudenbad who was famous for making items that were both helpful and harmful at the same time. Your bracelet is one of those items. Lose 1 SKILL point and gain 3 STAMINA points. Finding nothing else of interest, you set off again. Turn to **158**.

314

The Vampire Bat that bit you on the neck was riddled with tiny PARASITIC WORMS that burrow into the wound on your neck and infect you with a deadly virus. If you have a tin of Worm Paste, turn to **30**. If you do not have a tin of Worm Paste, turn to **187**.

315

An unseen assailant fires a small dart at you, which hits you in the neck. It's a poisoned dart, and the poison acts quickly. Roll one die and deduct the number rolled from your STAMINA points. If you are still alive, you hurry down the tunnel and don't stop until you reach the stone archway. If you left your sword in the wooden box, turn to **252**. If you are still carrying your sword, turn to **71**.

316

You stand on the slab and watch the Monk stand on slab 4, and finally the Thief who steps cautiously on to slab 5. Your heart begins to pound in your chest as you see Carnuss reach for an iron lever protruding from the wall of the cave entrance. The crowd goes silent when he takes hold of it with both hands. 'Contestants, you are about to enter my Dungeon of Despair. When I pull down on this lever, you will drop through the floor. I suppose I should warn you that one of you will not survive the fall! If any of you want to change places with another contestant, do so now!' The Thief raises his hand and says, 'I'll swap if anybody else will?' If you want to change places with Fingers, turn to **133**. If you want to stay where you are, turn to **75**.

317

You look to your left and see that the Assassin has been struck by another arrow, this time in the stomach. It doesn't stop her, and she runs at the Zanth Archers, ready to attack them with her spear. You charge at the archers who fired their arrows at you, striking the first one down before he has time to fire another arrow at you. You fight the other two one at a time.

First ZANTH ARCHER	SKILL 7	STAMINA 5
Second ZANTH ARCHER	SKILL 7	STAMINA 6

If you win, turn to **382**.

318

The itching becomes more intense as the bites turn red and angry and start to swell. You start to feel hot and realize you have got an infection. You sit down on the floor to rest, but it's not long before you break out into a fever. Lose 1 SKILL point and 4 STAMINA points. You roll over, unconscious, and when you wake up you discover that you have been robbed of all your Provisions and Gold Pieces (make a note on your *Adventure Sheet*). You stand up and look inside the chest and see a finely crafted breastplate made of polished steel. If you want to try on the breastplate, turn to **204**. If would rather walk back down the tunnel to the T-junction, turn to **33**.

319

As you go to draw your sword, the Juggler hurls one of his glass balls at the stone floor in front of you with a look of glee on his face. It smashes, releasing a cloud of blue gas that envelops you. Your head starts to spin, and you can't stop yourself from falling over and passing out. Lose 2 STAMINA points. When you wake up, the little man is nowhere to be seen. You stand up and notice that your backpack is open and some of your possessions are gone. Lose 1 LUCK point and remove five items from your *Adventure Sheet*. There is nothing you can do but curse the Juggler and choose which way to go. If you want to head west, turn 123. If you want to head east, turn 334.

320

You climb feet first into the chute and slide down, landing heavily on the rock floor of a tunnel below. Lose 1 STAMINA point. Wondering which way to head, you hear loud, stomping footsteps coming from east end of the tunnel. You draw your sword and stand ready to face the oncoming creature. Turn to **261**.

321

Tripping over the wire triggers small, needle-sharp iron spikes to shoot up from holes in the stone floor. You stumble forward in the darkness and step on a spike that goes through the sole of your boot and pierces your foot. Lose 2 STAMINA points. Once clear of the spikes, you walk on slowly, keeping an eye out for more traps. Turn to **62**.

322

You lift Thump's helmet off his head and see a gold key nestled in his thick hair with the number 180 stamped on it. You put it in your pocket and head north along the corridor. Turn to **6**.

323

Time passes slowly in the blistering heat, which is draining your energy. Lose 1 STAMINA point. All you can think about is having a long drink of cold water. You feel dizzy and dehydrated, but manage to stay on your feet without moving. Turn to **141**.

324

The Dragonmaster places three black dice on the table that have skulls on the faces instead of numbers. He calmly rolls his dice several times and says in a cold voice, 'The game we are about to play is the game of life. Your life. I roll my dice. You roll yours. Highest total wins. But, since this is the first test, I'm going to give you the chance to improve your dice roll. To do that, however, you will need to give me some charms. I collect charms, and I know there were four hidden in the dungeon. Did you find any? If you did, I suggest you place them on the table.' If you possess any charms and want to put them on the table, turn to **170**. If you want to tell the Dragonmaster that you do not have any charms, turn to **226**.

325

Picking your way through the candles, you walk over to the shield and lift it off the wall. It is sturdy and incredibly well made and looks like it will give you good protection in combat. You are holding a Sentinel Shield that has magic powers. Add 1 LUCK point. Add 1 point to your Attack Strength when using the shield in combat. If you have not done so already, you can take look at the helmet (turn to **139**) or, if you want to leave the room and continue walking up the tunnel, turn to **86**.

326

The Dragonmaster takes a key out from under his robes and unlocks the door. 'So near yet so far,' he says spitefully as he pushes the door open. You walk out into bright sunlight and find yourself at the top of a flight of stone steps with a huge crowd of people gathered at the bottom. They cheer loudly when they see you, but their cheers turn to jeers when they find out that you do not have the Golden Orb. You are pelted with rotten eggs and tomatoes and have to be rescued by the guards. You are marched to the harbour and put on a boat to take you back to the mainland. Your adventure is over.

327

When you reach the top of the steps, you see that the narrow passageway carries straight on. With the burning torches spaced far apart on the wall, it is difficult to see far ahead, but there is a door in the left-hand wall just a few metres away. You try to open it but find it is locked. There is a note pinned to the door that says 'Knock three times to enter'. If you want to knock on the door, turn to **353**. If you want to keep on walking, turn to **230**. If you want to go back down the staircase and turn right at the junction, turn to **265**.

A small creature is locked in an iron cage hanging from the ceiling

328

You head east along the tunnel with the sound of the bell getting noticeably louder. It leads into a cavern where you see a small iron cage suspended from the low ceiling by a thick rope. A small humanoid with long, pointed ears and a wild look in his eyes is sitting in the cage with his legs dangling out. He is holding a brass bell, and he looks very annoyed. Beyond the cage, you see there are two archways leading out of the cavern, one a continuation of the tunnel and the other a stairwell with spiral steps going up. When he sees you, the HOBGOBLIN starts banging the bell against the iron bars. 'You, human! Open cage!' he screams at the top of his voice. 'If help, me help.' If you want to help the Hobgoblin, turn to **161**. If you want to ignore him and walk over to the archways, turn to **393**.

329

You slide down the shaft and land in the new tunnel, unaware that your backpack is crawling with COCKROACHES. If you have any Provisions remaining, the Cockroaches gnaw their way through two of them before you notice and shake them out. Looking south, you see the tunnel ends almost immediately at a doorway. Looking north, you see a door in the right-hand wall some thirty metres ahead. If you want to open the door in the south wall, turn to **222**. If you want to head north, turn to **279**.

330

You place the ring on your finger, but don't sense it has magic powers. If you have not done so already, you can drink the liquid from the bottle (turn to **268**). If you do not want to drink the liquid, you can continue east (turn to **243**) or turn round and go back to the junction to head west (turn to **80**).

331

The corridor turns sharply left and you head east until you come to another door in the right-hand wall. You listen at the door, but do not hear anything. If you want to open the door, turn to **272**. If you want to carry on walking along the corridor, turn to **179**.

332

You search through your pockets and find the iron key you are looking for. The Gnome whoops for joy when you free him and gives you a Gold Piece as a reward. 'If you were thinking of going north, don't. There's a lethal trap up ahead.' If you want to carry on heading north, turn to **247**. If you want to take the Gnome's advice and turn round, turn to **375**.

333

You pass by an iron bucket hanging on a nail on the wall in which you find a silver coin with a crown embossed on one side and a dragon on the other side. Add 1 LUCK point. You put the coin in your pocket and walk on. It's not long before you arrive at a junction. Up ahead, you see there is a doorway in the left-hand wall of the tunnel. There is a narrow passageway in the right-hand wall that leads to a flight of stone steps going up. If you want to carry straight on, turn to **265**. If you want to walk down the passageway to the staircase, turn to **2**.

334

You walk quickly along the corridor to where it comes to a dead end some fifty metres down. There is a leather bag hanging by a cord on the end wall. The bag contains 2 Gold Pieces. Add 1 LUCK point. With the passageway at a dead end, you have no choice but to walk back to the junction and head west. Turn to **123**.

335

There is an eerie whooshing sound as a cloud of arrows flies across the arena, followed by the sickening thud of many of them hitting their target. There are loud oohs and aahs coming from the baying crowd as contestants fall to the ground, clutching the arrows lodged in their torsos. Roll two dice. If the total rolled is the same or less than your SKILL score, turn to **223**. If the total rolled is greater than your SKILL score, turn to **155**.

336

The Dragonmaster shakes his head and says solemnly, 'You have failed in your quest, but, thanks to the generosity of the great Lord Carnuss, your life will be spared for having reached this chamber.' The Dragonmaster pushes a lever down on the wall behind him, which opens a trapdoor in the floor above a chute. He gestures for you to slide down it and says, 'Freedom awaits you.' If you want to slide down the chute, turn to **214**. If you want to attack the Dragonmaster, turn to **38**.

337

You reach out and grab the handle. It doesn't turn, but you notice some words etched in the tail of one of the dragon engravings on the back of the door. If you want to read the words, turn to **203**. If you would rather walk over to the throne to pick up the Orb, turn to **228**.

338

The Zombie turns to dust on the floor, leaving behind nothing more than its manacles. If you have not done so already, you can either open the book entitled *Mages and Magic* (turn to **263**) or open the book entitled *Dungeon of Despair* (turn to **152**). If you want to leave the library and continue up the corridor, turn to **179**.

339

The Dwarf glares at you with contempt. 'Thanks a lot,' he says angrily as he barges past you. You decide to let him go on his way and continue walking along the tunnel. It's not long before you come to a dead end where a rockfall has blocked the passageway. There is nothing there except for the smouldering remains of a campfire, and all you can do is turn round and exit the tunnel. You are soon back at the copper mouth and turn right to head north up the passageway. Turn to **138**.

340

You pass by several more arrows chalked on the wall until the tunnel comes to a dead end. There is one more arrow on the end wall pointing down to a large wooden chest on the floor. If you want to open the chest, turn to **135**. If would rather walk back down the tunnel to the T-junction, turn to **33**.

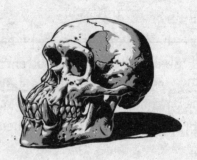

341

The Dragonmaster brings his arm forward and opens his hand. It is empty. 'You have failed in your quest, but, thanks to the generosity of the great Lord Carnuss, your life will be spared for being the first contestant to get to this point.' The Dragonmaster pushes a lever down on the wall behind him, which opens a trapdoor in the floor above a chute. He tells you to slide down the chute, adding, 'Freedom awaits you.' If you want to slide down the chute, turn to **214**. If you want to attack the Dragonmaster, turn to **38**.

342

The Thief looks disappointed that nobody wants to change places with him, but he shrugs his shoulders as though he doesn't care. The crowd gasps when Carnuss pulls down on the iron lever and the slabs fall away. You drop through a hole and find yourself sliding down a stone chute to land heavily at the bottom of a deep pit. Lose 1 STAMINA point. The pale light from amber crystals attached to the pit wall is just enough for you to see that the floor is covered in a writhing mass of SNAKES. There is a ladder attached to the pit wall that goes up to a wooden door higher up. If you want to fight the Snakes, turn to **189**. If you want to climb the ladder to open the door, turn to **110**.

343

You open the cupboards and chests, but find nothing except for a piece of paper tucked away at the back of one of the drawers. There is tiny handwriting on the paper that is so small that you are unable to read it. If you possess a magnifying glass, turn to **203**. If you do not possess a magnifying glass, turn to **11**.

344

Bronze is a metal that is an unbearable irritant to a Glugg. As soon as it is exposed to the bronze, the Glugg ejects you from its body. Add 1 LUCK point. You stand up and walk on, leaving the Glugg behind, and soon arrive at a junction. The new tunnel in the left-hand wall is narrow and has a very low ceiling. There is a putrid smell like rotten eggs coming from it and you decide to carry straight on. Turn to **115**.

345

The sword was forged long ago by a master swordsmith using the finest steel. You cut it through the air and marvel at its workmanship and fine balance. You have found a legendary Doom Sword. If you wish to take the Doom Sword, you must leave your own sword behind. If you have not done so already, you can either pick up the drawstring bag (turn to **24**) or, if you want to keep on walking, turn to **145**.

346

The Troll continues to insult you and lifts his spear in the air. You reach for your sword, but the Troll strikes before you can get hold of it. Your adventure is over.

347

You walk into the middle of the room and step warily on to the metal plate. It's solid and doesn't move. A monotone voice suddenly booms out from above. 'Welcome to the Room of Doom. The door is now locked. There is no other way out. One of the numbered boxes in front of you contains a key to unlock the door. You must now choose one box to open. And one box only. Do not open a second box.' You look at the boxes, which are numbered 1 to 3. Will you:

Open box No. 1?	Turn to **41**
Open box No. 2?	Turn to **132**
Open box No. 3?	Turn to **212**
Walk over to the door and try to open it?	Turn to **311**

A barefooted man approaches pointing a wooden staff

348

There is a T-junction up ahead where you see somebody run across, heading west. It's a bald, barefooted man who is carrying a wooden staff. He is wearing light brown robes tied at the waist, and his calves are bound with strips of cloth. It's Uzman Koh, the Monk. You hurry to the junction and call out his name. He stops and turns with a surprised look on his face. He walks slowly back towards you, watching you intently with his staff pointed at you. 'Hello, my friend,' he says calmly. 'Nothing personal. I'm just not taking any chances. I'm sure you understand. Everyone and everything is trying to kill me down here. Maybe we should team up? I'm heading west. Do you want to join me?' If you want to team up with the Monk, turn to **178**. If you want to decline his offer and tell him you are going to head east, turn to **240**.

349

With the Barbarian struggling to get back on his feet, you can't stop being pulled forward. Thump loses his footing and falls backwards, landing on the Priestess behind him. The Man-Orc yells at everybody to get back on the rope, but the chance to recover is gone. You continue to slide forward until the officer raises his sword to signal you have been dragged forward by a metre. The stone floor drops away beneath you, and you and your team fall into the void, screaming in terror. Your adventure is over.

350

You dive through the doorway just in time, with the heavy door slamming shut behind you. You try the handle, but it is firmly locked, and you have no option but to walk back along the passageway to the fire pit. When you enter the cave, you see the Lava Demon standing in your way. It scoops up a huge fistful of molten lava and hurls it at you. Its aim is deadly accurate. Your adventure is over.

351

The ceiling continues to grind its way down the walls, and there is nothing you can do to stop it. You try standing your sword upright on its tip on the floor, but the blade snaps under the weight of the ceiling. There is no way to escape being crushed. Your adventure is over.

352

The ravine is no more than two metres across. You throw your backpack and sword over the ravine and step back, ready to jump. You breathe in hard and run as fast as you can to jump over the ravine. You land safely on the other side and gather your belongings to carry on up the tunnel. Add 1 LUCK point. Turn to **174**.

353

As soon as you start to knock on the door, it flies open, and you are jumped on by a burly TROLL GUARD who lands a heavy blow on your head with a wooden club. If you are wearing a helmet, lose 1 STAMINA point. If you are not wearing a helmet, lose 2 STAMINA points. You stumble backwards against the opposite wall and try to clear your head as the Troll Guard raises his club to strike again. You must fight him.

TROLL GUARD   SKILL 7   STAMINA 6

If you win, turn to **245**.

354

You run to the Dwarf's aid and see there is a dagger sticking out of his back and blood seeping from his leather armour. He sees you and coughs. 'I didn't think I'd see you again,' he says slowly, spitting blood, his face contorted with pain. 'I'm done for. I'm not sure who did it. It could have been the ice-cold Assassin or that slime rat, Uzman Koh. I never trusted either of them.' His eyes suddenly widen as he draws in his last breath and slowly exhales. His head slumps forward and you realize there is nothing you can do for him. A quick search through his pockets yields 2 Gold Pieces and two charms, one a four-leaf clover and the other a small horseshoe. You put them in your pocket and head north along the corridor. Turn to **6**.

355

You draw your sword and ready yourself for combat. Three GIANT SEWER RATS emerge from the gloom and leap at you with their open jaws flashing long, needle-sharp teeth. You must fight the Sewer Rats one at a time.

First GIANT SEWER RAT	SKILL 5	STAMINA 4
Second GIANT SEWER RAT	SKILL 4	STAMINA 5
Third GIANT SEWER RAT	SKILL 5	STAMINA 5

If you win, turn to **88**.

356

You head east, leaving the Monk behind with the tunnel beginning to twist and turn. The floor is very uneven, and you have to watch your step to avoid tripping over. Looking down at the floor, you catch sight of something half buried under a rock that reflects the light of a burning torch on the wall. You reach down and pick up a stoppered bottle made of frosted glass. If you want to open the bottle, turn to **99**. If you want to put the bottle in your backpack and continue east, turn to **201**. If you want to go back and join the Monk, turn to **271**.

357

The Dragonmaster points a finger at you and says, 'You win. You have passed the first test, but now a tougher test awaits you. When you were exploring the dungeon, did you find any small metal balls bearing a dragon motif? They are Dragon Balls. If you have any, place them on the table.' If you possess Dragon Balls and wish to put them on the table, turn to **395**. If you want to tell the Dragonmaster that you do not have any, turn to **148**.

358

You walk over to the mirror and examine the frame and the fine detail of the snakes. When you look at the mirror, you feel a strange sensation on your face as though somebody is drawing a line down it. A jagged red line suddenly appears on your face, running from your forehead, over your left eye and down your cheek to your throat. The line turns into an ugly scar that looks exactly like the crack in the mirror. The mirror is cursed! You feel strangely weak, but there is nothing you can do to remove the Voodoo Scar. Lose 2 SKILL points and 2 LUCK points. If you haven't done so already, you can pick up the silver ring. Turn to **126**. If you would rather leave the room to walk up the corridor, turn to **331**.

359

You wipe the blood off the handle with a piece of cloth and open the door. Inside, you see a man in chain-mail armour lying face down on the floor. There is no sign of life. His broken sword and shield are lying by his side. If you want to search the body, turn to **185**. If you want to close the door and head north, turn to **154**.

360

You breathe in deeply and walk over to the door. You turn the key and hear the satisfying click of the lock mechanism turning. The Dragonmaster nods approvingly and says, 'A good start. Now you must select another key to unlock the second lock.' If you know which key to use, turn to the paragraph with the same number as the key. If you do not know which key to use, turn to **336**.

361

When all the contestants have teamed up with their partners, the officer announces with gusto, 'Bull's Eye is an archery contest! I hope you have chosen wisely because the targets for this contest are the contestants!' He sniggers, hardly able to contain himself. The spectators gasp in shock. The Pirate shakes his head and looks at you. 'Bah! Give me a cutlass any day,' he says despondently in a heavy accent. 'I've never fired a bow and arrow in my life, and I'm not going to start now. I'm quitting. Good luck to you. I hope you make it through.' He walks over to a guard who leads him unceremoniously out of the arena. There is a huge roar from the spectators when a trumpet blasts out a sharp note followed by the eerie whooshing sound of arrows flying across the arena, many of them hitting their targets. There are gasps from the crowd as contestants fall to the ground, clutching the arrows lodged in their torsos. Listening to the groans of the injured contestants, you are pleased to have missed this round. You scan the survivors and see Thump standing, hands on hips, with a big grin on his face. The trumpet blasts out again and the officer instructs the remaining contestants to line up against the wall opposite him while the injured are led out and the dead are dragged from the arena. You walk over to Thump and ask him what happened. 'I never learned how to use a bow and arrow so I figured that if I aimed to miss the Thug, I would be more likely to hit him. And I did!' he says, roaring with laughter. The officer looks along the line of contestants and says without any emotion in his voice, 'By my count, there are forty-eight contestants left in the tournament. Lord Carnuss requires that number to be reduced to twelve within the hour. It is time to choose a partner for the next contest. Do it now!' You agree with Thump's suggestion to split up, at least for now. If you want to choose the Thief on your left, turn to **98**. If you want to choose the Ninja on your right, turn to **184**.

A wounded Dwarf approaches armed with two short swords

362

You step into the demon's mouth and find yourself in a roughly hewn, twisting tunnel that has a very uneven floor. Watching where you step so as not to trip over, you walk round a bend and almost bump into somebody walking towards you. It is a Dwarf armed with two short swords. He is hunched over and looks to be in a bad way from his many wounds, which are bandaged with bloodstained strips of cloth. He eyes you suspiciously and says, 'Friend or foe?' If you want to reply 'Friend', turn to **273**. If you want to reply 'Foe', turn to **196**.

363

Your hand axe is sharp and sends large splinters of wood flying everywhere. You manage to cut a hole in the door big enough for you to climb through. You throw your backpack through the hole and dive after it with the ceiling just seconds away from touching the floor. Turn to **249**.

364

A figure appears at the top of the stairwell who looks surprised to see you. No more than a metre and a half tall, the ugly little creature has warty skin and long pointed ears, and is dressed in animal skins and odd bits of armour. It's a GOBLIN GUARD with another one behind him. The leading Goblin Guard reaches for his dagger and quickly throws it at you. *Test Your Luck*. If you are Lucky, turn to **59**. If you are Unlucky, turn to **281**.

365

You hear muffled cries for help coming from down the tunnel. You walk quickly on and soon arrive at an open doorway in the left-hand wall from where you can hear a female voice screaming, 'Help! Help!' It is a voice you have heard before! Turn to **29**.

366

You notice a slight incline in the tunnel floor that becomes gradually steeper as you walk along. There are carvings of skulls on the tunnel wall and one large carving of slaves dragging a huge dragon skull along a passageway. You walk on, with the steepness of the tunnel floor steadily increasing. You see a lever pointing upward in a slot in the right-hand wall. If you want to pull the lever down, turn to **57**. If you want to carry on walking uphill, turn to **312**.

367

Still breathing hard after fighting the Demon, you wade into the shallow water. With your eyes now adjusted to the gloom, you see there are steps leading up to the entrance to another tunnel on the left side of the cavern. You have no choice but to wade through the water over to the tunnel. *Test Your Luck*. If you are Lucky, turn to **9**. If you are Unlucky, turn to **134**.

368

Thump looks at you scornfully and says, 'Suit yourself.' Once outside, the officer leads you along a track lined with hundreds of cheering spectators. You soon arrive at a cave with its entrance surround carved into the shape of two fire-breathing dragons locked in battle. Standing there, waiting to greet you, is Lord Carnuss, resplendent in his purple robes. A huge crowd of people has gathered at the entrance, with everybody jostling for position, desperate to see the contestants close up. Carnuss motions for the crowd to hush so that he can be heard. 'I congratulate all six of you for getting this far. You are all heroes, but alas, there can only be one champion. I now want each of you to stand on one of the slabs on the ground here,' he says invitingly, pointing to six numbered stone slabs on in front of him. The Assassin makes her mind up quickly and stands on slab number 1, followed by Caldwell who steps confidently on to slab 3, and Thump who jumps on to slab 6. If you want to stand on slab 2, turn to **316**. If you want stand on slab 4, turn to **176**. If you want to stand on slab 5, turn to **40**.

369

You begin to feel unwell and double over with stomach cramps and nausea. You drop your sword and slump down on the floor, shivering and shaking, and pass out. You have drunk the Assassin's poison. Lose 8 STAMINA points. If you are still alive, turn to **121**.

370

Sliding the wooden panel open reveals a sunstone, set in a small mirrored box, that gives off powerful rays of white light. *Test Your Luck*. If you are Lucky, turn to **108**. If you are Unlucky, turn to **61**.

371

The man pockets your Gold Pieces and says, 'You will not be disappointed.' He turns and disappears into the crowd. You slide the knife into your belt and walk on to catch up with Thump. Turn to **12**.

372

You cut down several Snakes with your sword, but many more lunge at you to sink their poisonous fangs into your leg. Roll one die to determine how many of them bite you and reduce your STAMINA by 2 points for each bite. If you are still alive, turn to **63**.

373

You keep on walking and soon come to the edge of a deep pit. You think about jumping over it when you are suddenly pushed in the back. You fall head first into the pit and land heavily on a rocky floor. Lose 2 STAMINA points. You scramble to your feet and look up to see the Monk staring down at you with a smug grin on his face. 'Ha! Nobody ever hears me coming. You didn't. Thump didn't. Stealth is my gift, and I'm using it to win back the Golden Orb for Baron Sukumvit. He let me out of prison to compete here and promised me my freedom and 10,000 Gold Pieces if I returned the Orb to him. He even promised me a special reward if I eliminate Carnuss. And that's what I'm going to do. Enjoy yourself down there.' You watch the Monk leap silently across the pit and disappear. You realize that nobody was following you; it was just a ploy by the Monk to get you to walk ahead of him. The walls of the pit are smooth and impossible to climb, and a climbing rope is useless with nothing to tie it to. Time passes and you begin to think there is no way out of the pit when you hear a familiar voice from above. You look up and see it is the Assassin, Azurra Xang. 'Well, well, look who it is. What a surprise. It's so good to see you again,' she says sarcastically, smiling smugly. 'Now, remind me, what happened when you saw me trapped at the bottom of the Spider Pit?' If you helped the Assassin out of the pit, turn to **217**. If you did not help her, turn to **68**.

374

As he falls to the ground, the Woodcutter in his dying breath swings his axe at the clay pot, knocking it off the table. It smashes on the stone floor, and you see yellow gas rising from the broken pot. You grab his hand axe with gas beginning to fill the room. Your eyes start to water, your lungs feel like they are burning, and you start to cough uncontrollably. You fumble around, searching for the door handle, breathing in more poisonous gas before managing to escape from the room. Lose 1 SKILL point, 3 STAMINA points and 1 LUCK point. Still reeling from the effects of the gas, you stagger on up the corridor. Turn to **386**.

375

It doesn't take you long to get back to the junction where you continue straight on, heading east. The passageway soon makes a sharp left turn, and you walk north until you come to a tunnel in the right-hand wall that has an entrance in the shape of the head of a horned demon. It is made of copper that has turned bluish green with verdigris, and its open mouth is big enough to step through. There are burning torches on either side of the entrance and a large brass gong hanging in its wooden frame next to it. If you want to continue walking north, turn to **138**. If you want to enter the new tunnel, turn to **362**. If you want to ring the gong with the striker, turn to **92**.

376

The narrow torchlit passageway continues north for fifty metres before turning sharply right where you arrive at a staircase. You walk up the long flight of stone steps and, when you get to the top, you see that the passageway comes to a dead end twenty metres ahead. You walk on to the end of the passageway where you see arrows marked on the wall pointing downwards. You brush away loose sand and see that one of the stone slabs in the floor is hinged and has a small ring-pull handle fixed to it. You lift the slab up to find a tunnel directly below. There seems there is nothing else you can do but jump down. The new tunnel runs north to south. Looking north, you see that the tunnel soon ends at a doorway. There are burning torches on either side of the door, which you see is covered with deep scratch marks. Curious, you decide to investigate. Turn to **48**.

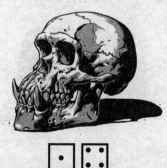

377

You stand opposite the Man-Orc, who grunts loudly when he catches your eye. The gates open and an ox-drawn cart piled high with large iron balls rolls slowly into the arena. The officer instructs everybody to take an iron ball from the cart and stand holding it above their head opposite their partner. The ball is heavy, and you have difficulty in lifting it above your head. Snarling and snorting to focus on the task, the Man-Orc has no trouble lifting his ball. Your arms soon start to ache. The crowd cheers as iron balls thud into the ground all around the arena with the eliminated contestants led away by the guards. The muscles in your arms tremble under the weight of the ball, and you wonder how much longer you can last. Lose 2 STAMINA points. You glare at the sweating Man-Orc, whose gritted teeth and wide-eyed expression tell you that he is also beginning to feel the strain. Turn to **149**.

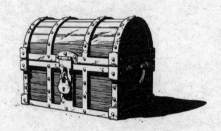

378

You slide down the rope for a few seconds before landing on a solid stone floor in near pitch-black darkness. You cannot see anything, but hear the faint sound of flapping wings and realize there are creatures flying round your head. Something bites you on the neck, which you brush away with your hand. You feel blood trickling down your neck. Lose 1 STAMINA point. When your eyes to adjust to the dark, you see three VAMPIRE BATS circling the cavern you are standing in. You draw your sword and must fight them one at a time.

First VAMPIRE BAT	SKILL 5	STAMINA 5
Second VAMPIRE BAT	SKILL 5	STAMINA 6
Third VAMPIRE BAT	SKILL 6	STAMINA 5

If you win, turn to **280**.

Smoke billows from the Dragon's nostrils as it roars and belches fire

379

When you place the Dragon Ball on the table, the Dragonmaster says in a condescending voice, 'Finding only one Dragon Ball is pitiful. Because of that, you have a very daunting task ahead of you. Follow me.' He walks over to the first iron door in the left-hand wall and unlocks it. He opens the door and beckons you to walk through, saying, 'If you survive, knock on the door. I'll be waiting for you.' You draw your sword and walk into a huge cave. You hear the door slam shut behind you and stare in disbelief at the size of the RED DRAGON standing threateningly in the middle of the cavern. Its torso is covered with thick red scales and it has huge dark red wings. Smoke billows from its nostrils. It sees you and roars, belching fire so close to you that you feel the heat from it on your face. You must fight the young fire-breathing Dragon.

RED DRAGON	*SKILL* 11	*STAMINA* 16

If you win, turn to **32**.

380

The dagger strikes you painfully in the thigh, causing a deep wound. Lose 2 STAMINA points. You pull it out of your leg and slide it into your belt and attend to your wound. You walk over to the shelf at the back of the room with Xang screaming angrily at you. 'You'll regret this!' she shouts. 'May the Fireworms of Slann burn through your eyeballs!' Ignoring her wrath, you look inside the silver chalice and find a small solid silver ball that is etched with a dragon motif. You place both items in your backpack and leave the room to carry on up the tunnel with the Assassin still cursing you loudly. Turn to **124**.

381

The Dragonmaster tells you to put the keys down on the table. He picks up one of them, taps the table with it and says, 'You have done well to find all four Compass Keys. Lord Carnuss did not think it would be possible. You will see that the door behind me has four keyholes in it. These must be unlocked in strict order from top to bottom. Choose a key to open the top lock.' If you know which key to use, turn to the paragraph with the same number as the key. If you do not know which key to use, turn to **336**.

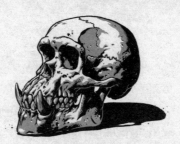

382

You look over to the Assassin and watch her despatch the final archer. She drops to her knees, holding her stomach, with blood oozing out between her fingers. She looks at you through half-open eyes and shakes her head, knowing there is no hope for her. She rolls over on her side and goes limp. 'Lost your friend, have you? What a shame,' you hear a familiar voice say sarcastically from the back of the chamber. A figure steps out of the shadows who you recognize instantly. It's Uzman Koh! 'I didn't think I would see you again. Who is going to save you now?' he says, sneering. 'The answer is nobody!' He runs towards you at speed, leaps into the air and does a double backflip, landing almost on top of you. He spins round and lunges at you with his staff. You must fight the Monk! Unless you are wearing a silver armband, you will find it hard to focus on the Monk's agile movements and must reduce your Attack Strength by 1 point during this battle.

MONK   *SKILL* 10   *STAMINA* 8

If you win, turn to **209**.

383

You tentatively slide the ring on to your middle finger, half expecting something to happen. You do not feel any different, but, unbeknownst to you, you are wearing a Ring of Ill Fortune. Lose 3 LUCK points. Unaware that the ring is cursed, you put the box back on the ledge and walk over to the iron door to open it. Turn to **251**.

384

You hit the floor with the bulk of the lava flying overhead, but a small lump of it lands on your arm. The pain is intense, but you manage to scrape the lava off with your sword to prevent yourself being too badly burned. Lose 3 STAMINA points. As the Lava Demon reaches down to pick up more lava, you seize your chance and run as fast as you can along the pathway round the fire pit into the new tunnel. Turn to **129**.

385

When you lift the lid, your nostrils are filled with the terrible stench coming from the rotten meat stored inside the chest. A cloud of BLACK FLY swarms out of the chest and buzzes round your head. You hold your breath and drop the lid, but cannot avoid being stung by the Black Fly as they fly out of the room. Lose 1 STAMINA point. If you have not done so already, you can either eat the food on the table (turn to **168**) or try to open the door at the back of the room (turn to **67**). If you would rather leave the room and head north up the passageway, turn to **230**. If you want to leave the room and run back down the staircase and turn right at the junction, turn to **265**.

386

You soon arrive at another door in the left-hand wall of the tunnel. You listen at the door, but do not hear anything. If you want to enter the room, turn to **229**. If you want to keep walking, turn to **86**.

387

You breathe in deeply and put your hands slowly under the Golden Orb to lift it up. It is solid gold and heavy. You are convinced it is the fabled treasure. While you are busy packing it away in your backpack, one of the fingers drops off the stone hand and lands on top of the plinth. You hear a hissing sound and see gas escaping from where the finger broke off from the hand. You rush over to the bronze door and strike the knocker against the door. Long flames shoot out from the dragon's mouth and burn you. Roll one dice and reduce your STAMINA points by the number rolled. If you are still alive, turn to **127**.

388

The monotone voice booms out again the moment you touch the box lid. 'The instruction was to open one box only. You must suffer the consequences of your action.' The iron plate in the middle of the room slowly rises to reveal a large hole from which hundreds of small, venomous SCORPIONS crawl out with their large stingers raised. You do your best to fend them off, but one of them stings you. Lose 2 STAMINA points. You feel weak from the effects of the poison and stagger over to the door and put the key in the lock only to find that the door isn't locked. You stamp angrily on a Scorpion and leave the room to head west along the tunnel. Turn to **198**.

389

There is an eerie whooshing sound of arrows flying across the arena, many of them hitting their targets, including you. The High Elf's arrow sinks into your left thigh, making you scream out in pain. A guard grabs your arm and drags you out of the arena with no concern for your injury. You look back and see the High Elf leaning on her bow, waving at you with a smirk on her face. You can hardly believe that you are out of the contest so soon. Your adventure is over.

390

You sit down on the bench and watch him juggle his glass balls. 'Have a nap. I'll wake you if a monster appears!' he says jovially. You are soon fast asleep and, when you wake, the little man is nowhere to be seen. The sleep has revived you and given you some much-needed energy. Add 2 STAMINA points. When you stand up, you notice that your backpack is open and some of your possessions are gone. Lose 1 LUCK point and remove five items from your *Adventure Sheet*. There is nothing you can do but curse the Juggler and choose which way to go. If you want to head west, turn to **123**. If you want to head east, turn to **334**.

391

As you climb up the next step, the Ghost-Witch's eyes widen, and she lets out a high-pitched screech that echoes down the passageway. She glides down the staircase and reaches out with a bony hand that passes through you as though you are a ghost yourself. You feel a sudden chill, and a sensation like an ice-cold hand squeezing your heart. Lose 1 SKILL point and 5 STAMINA points. If you are still alive, you watch the Ghost-Witch glide along the passageway and disappear left round the corner. If you want to climb to the top of the staircase, turn to **327**. If you want to go back down the steps and turn right at the junction, turn to **265**.

392

The door opens into a narrow corridor with a polished stone floor and smooth walls. There are paintings on the walls running the length of the corridor. All the paintings are of Baron Sukumvit being attacked by hideous creatures. There is a door in the left-hand wall halfway down the corridor, and another door at the end. If you want to open the door on the left, turn to **51**. If you want to open the door at the end of the corridor, turn to **309**.

393

You peer into the tunnel heading east out of the cavern and see it is narrow and gloomy. You peer into the second archway and look up the staircase, but can't see anything unusual. If you want to walk down the tunnel, turn to **207**. If you want to climb the spiral staircase, turn to **238**.

They are deadly bowmen from the Southern Plains

394

You breathe in deeply and pull both doors open. You charge into the chamber together, screaming at the top of your voice. For a moment, it looks like there is nobody in the chamber, but suddenly six lanky creatures with pointed heads and long teeth jump out from behind the stone columns. They are ZANTH ARCHERS, deadly bowmen hired in from the Southern Plains. They take aim with their longbows and let fly their arrows at you. If you are carrying a shield, turn to **191**. If you are not carrying a shield, turn to **266**.

395

The Dragonmaster watches you carefully as you reach into your backpack and says, 'How many Dragon Balls do you have?' Will you reply:

One	Turn to **379**
Two	Turn to **84**
Three	Turn to **276**
Four	Turn to **107**
Five	Turn to **193**

396

As you turn to walk away, she throws a dagger at you in anger. *Test Your Luck*. If you are Lucky, turn to **190**. If you are Unlucky, turn to **380**.

397

You discover a tin in one of the drawers that rattles when you shake it. You prise the lid off and find a gold key with the number 90 stamped on it. Pleased with your find, you walk over to the door to leave the room. Turn to **82**.

398

You run across the chalk line with Thump and five others. With the teams established, a party of scrawny slaves enters the arena, carrying shovels. They begin digging out the sand on both sides of the white line to reveal two long sections of solid stone floor. When they are finished, more slaves enter the arena, carrying a long length of thick rope. They lay it lengthways across both sections of the stone floor with half of it on one side of the chalk line and half of it on the other side. 'A Line in the Sand is a Tug-of-War contest. It will be the final contest in the arena,' the officer announces triumphantly to rapturous applause from the crowd. 'Take your positions on the rope.' Your team members look at each other before the tall Barbarian says in a gruff voice, 'I should be the lead puller.' 'And I should be the anchor,' the Priestess says, smiling. 'Why you? I am stronger than you. I should be the anchor,' the Man-Orc says dismissively. 'You'll see,' the Priestess replies calmly. 'Let's vote on it,' says Thump, and everybody agrees. If you want to vote for the Priestess to be the anchor, turn to **130**. If you want to vote for the Man-Orc to be the anchor, turn to **278**.

399

It's not long before you arrive at another junction. The new tunnel in the left-hand wall is narrow and has a very low ceiling. There is a putrid smell like rotten eggs coming from the entrance and you decide to carry straight on. Turn to **115**.

400

You find yourself at the top of a flight of stone steps, staring down at a huge gathering of people standing at the bottom who are waving and cheering loudly. The sunlight is very bright, and it takes a few moments to get used to it. You hold the Golden Orb in the air, which makes the crowd cheer even louder. Suddenly the cheers turn to whispers. The crowd parts, and you see Lord Carnuss approach with his bodyguards at his side and his entourage walking behind him. He stops and looks up at the Gatekeeper who is standing next to you. The Gatekeeper nods once, and Lord Carnuss beckons you to join him. You walk down the steps to stand facing Lord Carnuss, who stares at you fiercely. 'Congratulations,' he says through gritted teeth. 'You have done well to survive my dungeon. You are a true champion. Your prize is one of the greatest treasures in Allansia.' He shakes your hand firmly and leans forward to whisper in your ear, 'I only hope you live long enough to enjoy it.' You smile and hand him the handwritten note from Baron Sukumvit. He looks stunned when he reads it. He looks up and says, 'I didn't expect anyone to win through today, but it is my good fortune that it was you who did. My brother must pay for his treachery with his life. You have proved yourself to be an elite Adventurer so might I interest you in a little assignment in Fang? I'm sure my brother would be delighted to see you. Give it some thought, but not for too long since I will not take no for an answer. But we can talk again tomorrow. This day belongs to you.' He smiles and waves to the happy crowd before leaving with his bodyguards and attendants. You are hoisted on to the shoulders of two tall men and carried through the throng of people, who cheer loudly as you pass through them. Your mind spins with thoughts of what destiny the Orb will bring you, but tonight will be a night of joy and celebration.

HOW TO FIGHT
THE CREATURES IN THE
DUNGEON ON BLOOD ISLAND

YOU have been preparing for your quest by practising your swordplay and building up your strength and STAMINA. You possess a sword and a backpack containing Provisions (food and drink) to help sustain you during your adventure. Before setting off, you must first roll dice to record your SKILL, STAMINA and LUCK scores on your *Adventure Sheet* on pages 260–271, which you should also use to keep a record of the items you find on your adventure. Use the adjacent *Monster Encounter Boxes* to record combat with monsters during the adventure. Write your scores in pencil or make photocopies of the blank *Adventure Sheet* and *Monster Encounter Boxes* to use in future adventures.

SKILL, STAMINA AND LUCK

To determine your Initial SKILL, STAMINA and LUCK scores:

- Roll one die. Add 6 to this number and enter this total in the SKILL box on the *Adventure Sheet*.
- Roll two dice. Add 12 to the number rolled and enter this total in the STAMINA box.
- Roll one die. Add 6 to this number and enter this total in the LUCK box.

SKILL reflects your swordsmanship and fighting expertise; the higher the better. STAMINA represents your strength; the higher your STAMINA, the longer you should survive. LUCK represents how lucky a person you are; the higher your LUCK score, the luckier you will be.

SKILL, STAMINA and LUCK scores increase and decrease during an adventure, and you must keep an accurate record of them. Although you may gain additional SKILL, STAMINA and LUCK points during the adventure, your Initial levels may never be exceeded unless special instructions are given.

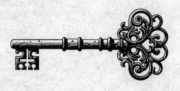

BATTLES

When you are told to fight a creature, you must resolve the battle as described below in a series of Attack Rounds. First, write down the enemy's SKILL and STAMINA scores in an empty *Monster Encounter Box* on the *Adventure Sheet* and make a note of your own SKILL and STAMINA scores. The sequence of combat is then:

1. Roll the two dice for your enemy and add the total to their SKILL score. This is your enemy's Attack Strength.

2. Roll the two dice for yourself and add the total your current SKILL. This is your Attack Strength. Whose Attack Strength is higher? If your Attack Strength is higher, you have wounded your enemy – go to 4. If the enemy's Attack Strength is higher, it has wounded you – go to 5. (If both are the same, you have both missed – start the next Attack Round from step 1 above.)

3. If you wounded your enemy, subtract 2 points from the enemy's STAMINA score. You may use LUCK here to do additional damage (see 'Using Luck in Battles' below).

4. If your enemy wounded you, subtract 2 points from your STAMINA score. You may use LUCK to minimize the damage (see 'Using LUCK in Battles' below).

5. Make the appropriate changes to either the creature's or your own STAMINA scores (and your LUCK score if you used LUCK) and begin the next Attack Round (repeat steps 1–6).

6. This continues until the STAMINA score of either you or the creature you are fighting has been reduced to zero (death).

7. This continues until the STAMINA score of either you or the creature you are fighting has been reduced to zero (death).

ESCAPING

During certain battles you will be given the option to Escape. If you think you are going to be defeated, you may Escape, but you must lose 2 STAMINA points, as your opponent is deemed to have wounded you as you flee.

LUCK

At various times during your adventure, you will be told to *Test Your Luck*. LUCK plays a part in deciding what happens to you.

HOW TO TEST YOUR LUCK

Roll two dice. If the number rolled is equal to or less than your current LUCK score, you have been Lucky. If the number rolled is higher than your current LUCK score, you have been Unlucky. The consequences of being Lucky or Unlucky will be found in the paragraph you are sent to. Each time you *Test Your Luck*, you must subtract one point from your current LUCK score. The more you rely on luck, the riskier this becomes.

USING LUCK IN BATTLES

During combat, you have the option of using your LUCK either to score a more serious wound on a creature, or to minimize the effects of a wound the creature has just scored on you.

If you wounded the creature: you may *Test Your Luck* as described above. If you are Lucky, subtract an extra

2 points from the creature's STAMINA score (i.e. 4 instead of 2 normally). But if you are Unlucky, you must restore 1 point to the creature's STAMINA (so, instead of causing 2 points of damage, you have only caused 1).

If you were wounded by the creature: you may *Test Your Luck* to try to minimize the wound. If you are Lucky, restore 1 point of your STAMINA (i.e., instead of causing 2 points of damage, it has only caused 1). If you are Unlucky, subtract 1 extra STAMINA point.

Don't forget to subtract 1 point from your LUCK score each time you *Test Your Luck*.

RESTORING SKILL, STAMINA AND LUCK

SKILL

Occasionally, an event may alter your SKILL score. For example, a Magic Sword may increase your SKILL, but remember that only one weapon can be used at a time. You cannot claim 2 SKILL bonuses for carrying two Magic Swords.

Drinking the Potion of Skill (see 'Potions' below) will restore your SKILL to its Initial level.

STAMINA AND PROVISIONS

Your STAMINA score will change a lot during the adventure. As you near your goal, your STAMINA level may be dangerously low, so be careful!

You start the game with enough Provisions for ten meals. You may only eat one meal at a time. When you have a meal, add 4 points to your STAMINA score and reduce your Provisions total by one. Keep a record of your Provisions in the box provided on the *Adventure Sheet*. Remember to use your Provisions wisely.

Drinking the Potion of Strength (see 'Potions' below) will restore your STAMINA to its Initial level.

LUCK

Your LUCK score will change during your adventure. For example, you may find a lucky charm that adds to your LUCK score. Or an evil spell might reduce your LUCK score.

Drinking the Potion of Luck (see 'Potions' below) will restore your LUCK to its Initial level.

POTIONS

You begin your adventure with a sword and a backpack containing Provisions (food and drink). You will find gold, treasure, weapons, armour and artefacts on your adventure. But not all items will help you on your quest. Some might even harm you!

You may also take a Magic Potion, which will aid you on your quest. Each bottle of potion contains enough for one measure, i.e. it can only be used once during an adventure. Choose ONE of the following:

- A Potion of Skill restores SKILL points to their Initial level

- A Potion of Stamina restores STAMINA points to their Initial level

- A Potion of Luck restores LUCK points to their Initial level

These potions may be taken at any time during the adventure, but not during combat.

HINTS ON PLAY

There is 'one true way' through *The Dungeon on Blood Island* and it will probably take you several attempts to find it. Making notes and drawing a map as you explore will help you on your quest.

Not all locations contain treasure. Some contain deadly traps and creatures. There are several 'wild goose chase' passages and, while you may progress through to your ultimate destination, winning is not guaranteed.

The 'one true way' involves a minimum of risk and, even with low Initial dice rolls, you should be able to win through.

Good luck on your adventure and may your STAMINA never fail!

ALTERNATIVE DICE

If you do not have a pair of dice to hand, dice rolls are printed throughout the book at the bottom of the pages. Flicking rapidly through the book and stopping on a page will give you a random dice roll. If you need to 'roll' only one die, use the number on the first die. If you need to roll two dice, use the total of both dice.

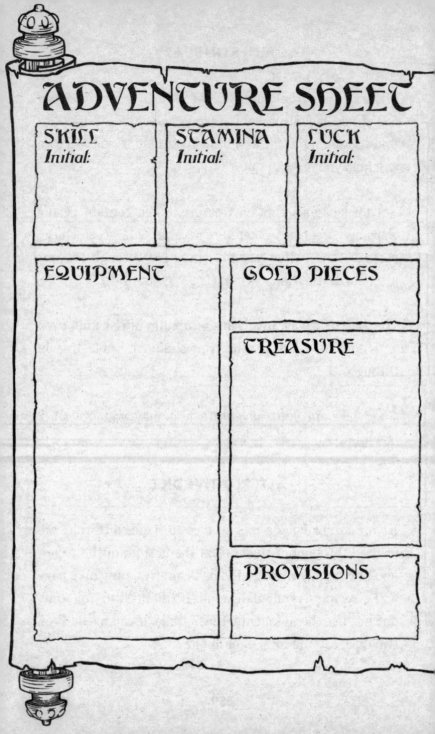

ADVENTURE SHEET

SKILL	STAMINA	LUCK
Initial:	Initial:	Initial:

EQUIPMENT

GOLD PIECES

TREASURE

PROVISIONS

MONSTER ENCOUNTER BOXES

Skill: Stamina:	Skill: Stamina:	Skill: Stamina:
Skill: Stamina:	Skill: Stamina:	Skill: Stamina:
Skill: Stamina:	Skill: Stamina:	Skill: Stamina:
Skill: Stamina:	Skill: Stamina:	Skill: Stamina:

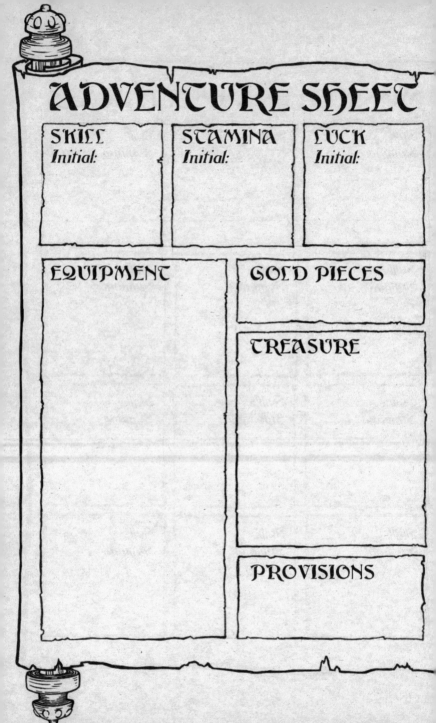

ADVENTURE SHEET

SKILL
Initial:

STAMINA
Initial:

LUCK
Initial:

EQUIPMENT

GOLD PIECES

TREASURE

PROVISIONS

MONSTER ENCOUNTER BOXES

Skill: *Stamina:*	*Skill:* *Stamina:*	*Skill:* *Stamina:*
Skill: *Stamina:*	*Skill:* *Stamina:*	*Skill:* *Stamina:*
Skill: *Stamina:*	*Skill:* *Stamina:*	*Skill:* *Stamina:*
Skill: *Stamina:*	*Skill:* *Stamina:*	*Skill:* *Stamina:*

ADVENTURE SHEET

SKILL
Initial:

STAMINA
Initial:

LUCK
Initial:

EQUIPMENT

GOLD PIECES

TREASURE

PROVISIONS

MONSTER ENCOUNTER BOXES

Skill: *Stamina:*	*Skill:* *Stamina:*	*Skill:* *Stamina:*
Skill: *Stamina:*	*Skill:* *Stamina:*	*Skill:* *Stamina:*
Skill: *Stamina:*	*Skill:* *Stamina:*	*Skill:* *Stamina:*
Skill: *Stamina:*	*Skill:* *Stamina:*	*Skill:* *Stamina:*

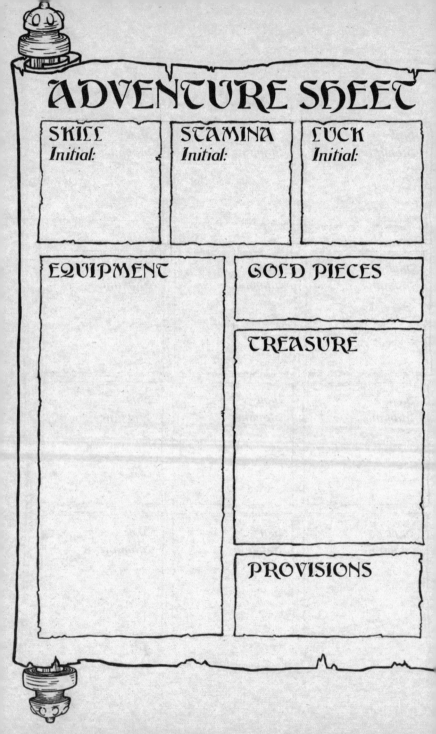

ADVENTURE SHEET

SKILL
Initial:

STAMINA
Initial:

LUCK
Initial:

EQUIPMENT

GOLD PIECES

TREASURE

PROVISIONS

MONSTER ENCOUNTER BOXES

Skill: *Stamina:*	*Skill:* *Stamina:*	*Skill:* *Stamina:*
Skill: *Stamina:*	*Skill:* *Stamina:*	*Skill:* *Stamina:*
Skill: *Stamina:*	*Skill:* *Stamina:*	*Skill:* *Stamina:*
Skill: *Stamina:*	*Skill:* *Stamina:*	*Skill:* *Stamina:*

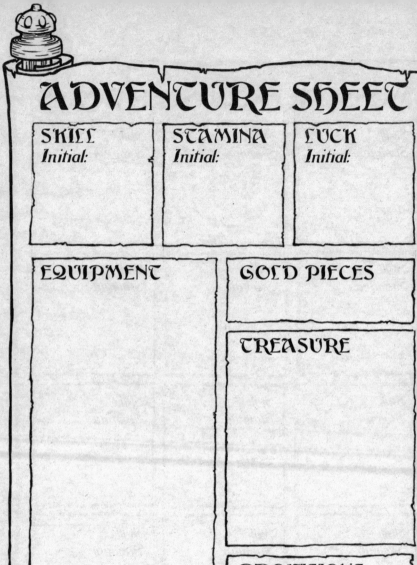

ADVENTURE SHEET

SKILL
Initial:

STAMINA
Initial:

LUCK
Initial:

EQUIPMENT

GOLD PIECES

TREASURE

PROVISIONS

MONSTER ENCOUNTER BOXES

Skill: *Stamina:*	*Skill:* *Stamina:*	*Skill:* *Stamina:*
Skill: *Stamina:*	*Skill:* *Stamina:*	*Skill:* *Stamina:*
Skill: *Stamina:*	*Skill:* *Stamina:*	*Skill:* *Stamina:*
Skill: *Stamina:*	*Skill:* *Stamina:*	*Skill:* *Stamina:*

ADVENTURE SHEET

SKILL
Initial:

STAMINA
Initial:

LUCK
Initial:

EQUIPMENT

GOLD PIECES

TREASURE

PROVISIONS

MONSTER ENCOUNTER BOXES

Skill: Stamina:	Skill: Stamina:	Skill: Stamina:
Skill: Stamina:	Skill: Stamina:	Skill: Stamina:
Skill: Stamina:	Skill: Stamina:	Skill: Stamina:
Skill: Stamina:	Skill: Stamina:	Skill: Stamina: